caroline murphy

Photography by Ray Main

101 IDEAS
bathrooms

BARNES
& NOBLE
BOOKS
NEW YORK

This edition published by Barnes & Noble, Inc. by arrangement with Quadrille Publishing Ltd.

2004 Barnes & Noble books

M 10 9 8 7 6 5 4 3 2 1

ISBN 0-7607-6146-9

Editorial Director Jane O'Shea
Art Director Helen Lewis
Designer Paul Welti
Project Editor Hilary Mandleberg
Production Jane Rogers

Photography Ray Main

Printed in China

contents

part one
the big picture

part one

the big picture

1 bathroom basics

10 elements

Designing a bathroom may seem a daunting task. The technicalities of plumbing, worries about waterproofing, the upheaval of structural change . . . there are so many practical matters to consider. Yet simultaneously, designing a bathroom can be fun. Imagine making that "if I won the lottery . . ." wish list, poring over magazines featuring beautiful bathrooms, unleashing creative instincts you never knew you had. You could really enjoy the rewarding visual aspects of bathroom design (and leave the complex technical side to the experts).

But your finished bathroom will be so much more successful as a functional room if you have a sound understanding of the practicalities behind different elements of the design. Getting back to basics and questioning every choice you make ("What are the benefits of a big bathtub?" "What exactly do I need to store?" "Where would lights work best?") will ensure that a perfect balance between form and function is achieved.

bathtub

Generally, size will be the first consideration, closely followed by color, material, and shape (see 27–33). Be realistic about what will suit your bathroom. Even a modest-sized bathtub can be luxurious, fitted with whirlpool jets and with a powerful overhead shower (see 34).

shower

Do you know your water pressure and how your hot water is produced? Without these vital facts, you won't be able to choose the best shower for your needs (see 37). The style of the shower-head, the shape of the enclosure, and the size of the base are all secondary to the water flow (see 38–45).

sink

Where should I put my sink? How should I mount it? What kind of use will it get? These are the questions you should be asking yourself, in addition to exploring the benefits of ceramic versus glass, or stone troughs versus wooden bowls (see 46–52).

faucets

Polished chrome or matte steel, old-fashioned brass or warm nickel? Whichever faucets you choose, they should look good as well as being durable, and they need to be easy to use, too. Can you turn them with soapy hands, for example? (See 53–56.)

the toilet

Not a glamorous subject, but one that deserves some thought. Think about comfort and hygiene, as well as design tricks like concealing the cistern or attaching the bowl to the wall (see 13 and 58). You might consider separating the toilet from the bathroom, as is sometimes done in Europe (see 60).

storage

If you use the bare minimum of toiletries and a few cleaning agents, you'll obviously need less storage than someone who revels in bottles galore and piles of towels. Make sure the furniture you choose— whether a medicine cabinet, display shelves, or banks of furniture—will be purposeful (see 62–67).

walls

How you finish your walls depends on personal taste and budget, from a quick slick of paint to painstaking tiling with tumbled marble mosaics (see 69–75). Don't be afraid to mix different surfaces so you get the waterproofing you need and the look you want (see 68).

floors

Beneath your feet, but not beneath your notice, a bathroom floor covering needs to be non-slip, comfortable for bare feet, and, of course, waterproof (see 76). Compare the maintenance issues as well as the aesthetics of ceramic, stone, vinyl, and wood (see 77–82).

lighting

Use light to decorate as much as to illuminate, with wall-washers, downlights, and uplights creating mood and dimension in the bathroom. For practical purposes make sure there's sufficient light where it's really needed—by the mirror, for example (see 83–86).

heating

In the room where warmth matters most, heating is vital. If you want underfloor heating, you'll have to explore it at an early stage of the design, unless you want to re-lay your floor; and positioning of radiators, if any, is crucial (see 87–90).

getting inspiration

2

If you're bereft of creative ideas in terms of color and style, or struggling to imagine a new layout, don't despair: sources of inspiration can be found all around you.

showrooms

Some showrooms offer row after uninspiring row of bathtubs, sinks, and faucets, but the better ones will show off their products in lifelike displays. Within one showroom you may find 10 or 20 different bathroom looks, which will help you imagine how your own completed bathroom could appear.

catalogs

Order a stack of bathroom catalogs via the Internet or by calling the hotline numbers on ads. As well as technical information about a particular company's collections, there are pictures of the products in beautifully styled room sets, which will allow you to see the potential of your own room.

magazines

Interior design magazines offer a glimpse into other people's homes, helping you imagine what you can achieve with your own bathroom. Cut out the pictures you like, and keep a folder for useful names and numbers.

television

There is a plethora of home-decorating programs on television, showing the transformation of shabby rooms into splendid spaces. Featuring all stages of design, from gutting a room to accessorizing, they encourage you to see that dream designs can be realized. Expect your own renovation to take longer than 24 hours, though!

other people's bathrooms

Besides taking careful note of friends' bathrooms, you should also pay attention to restrooms in restaurants and bars, as well as hotel bathrooms—you'll often see exciting design innovations used in commercial spaces.

likes and dislikes

One of the best—and easiest—ways to start planning a new bathroom is to think about how you use your old one. Stand in it with a pen and paper in hand and answer the following questions:

♥ **What's the best thing about the bathroom?**

✗ **What's the worst part of it?**

♥ **What looks good—but is impractical?**

✗ **What looks ugly—but is useful?**

♥ **Is there anything you don't want to change?**

You might think that the good natural light is the best thing; the small space is the worst; the shiny chrome faucet looks good but shows watermarks; the radiator looks terrible but is great for hanging towels; and you couldn't bear to change your large window. This gives you a starting point: you want to maximize space and make the most of the light from the window. You might want to consider a matte chrome faucet that won't show watermarks, and to change your radiator for a towel-warming rail, which will provide heat as well as a place to hang (and warm) your towels.

Asking your partner—and even your children—for their opinions will help you create a plan of attack and will highlight common likes and dislikes.

Make a scrapbook, including pictures from magazines and brochures. Collect samples of tiles, paint colors, and fabric swatches to show the textures, colors, and materials you like. Also keep a folder of things you don't like— this is especially important if you are commissioning an interior designer to help create your bathroom. They'll need to know what to avoid as much as what to include.

money matters

The often-raised question "How much does a new bathroom cost?" is as unanswerable as the age-old "How long is a piece of string?" Innumerable factors influence the costs, with perhaps the most important being how much you are prepared to spend.

five budgeting steps

1 • Set a budget. Ask yourself how much you can afford and what a new bathroom is worth to you. Do you have any savings you can dip into, or will you have to take out a loan? Be realistic.

2 • Estimate costs. Visit showrooms and look at price lists in catalogs. Add up the cost of every element in your design, and don't forget wall and floor finishes, faucets, lighting, and heating. Add about 25% onto that total to pay for installation.

3 • Channel the money. Think about how best to apportion your pot of money. You could cut out installation costs by doing it yourself, but unless you're skilled, it could be a disaster. Shop around for bargains; unbranded products usually cost less, and if you save on the sink and toilet, you could spend more on a big and sturdy bathtub. Don't be tempted to skimp on "moving parts" like faucets and the shower, though. Cheaper versions are more likely to break and may not be guaranteed.

4 • Ascertain the schedule of payments. When will you have to pay? Designers may request a deposit in advance. On-site contractors may expect weekly payments. And some retailers may allow you to pay in installments for their goods. Make sure your cash flow can cope with all demands.

5 • Include a contingency fund. Things go wrong, delays occur, and they always cost you money. . . You need to allow for the unexpected. Set aside 5–10% above your budget for any contingencies.

should you do it yourself?

5

Some see home improvement as a satisfying hobby or an exciting challenge, but to many others, it's a last resort. A tight budget is one of the main reasons for the hands-on approach to remodeling, but whatever your motivation, are you prepared for the work?

If it's a question of simply repainting walls to update a tired décor, any reasonably competent person can master it. Check out a home improvement manual for advice on preparing walls beforehand, and get advice in the store about the type of paint you're buying. Jobs such as plastering and tiling take a degree of expertise to complete them correctly, but with practice (and that trusty manual), you could succeed.

When it comes to plumbing and electricity, though, it's best to step aside for the professionals. (In some cases, it's even illegal for a non-qualified person to undertake the work.)

Mistakes with pipes and wiring can be not only costly but also dangerous, so save up the money—or put your pride aside—and get the experts involved.

where to start?

There are plenty of books to turn to, plus helpful websites and forums where like-minded beginners and enthusiasts are happy to answer specific queries. (Type "bathroom design," a string of relevant words, or even your specific query into a search engine.) Ask advice in the store you buy the products from; the sales assistants may be knowledgeable or may have brochures to help you. It's true that most products will come with their own set of instructions, but unless you're experienced, you'll probably find the technical guides practically incomprehensible.

6 bathroom designers

Designing a bathroom is easier than you may think: it's a matter of planning a layout, choosing the products to fit, and deciding on a decorative look. There are so many sources of inspiration—and guides, such as this book—that with some research and hard work, even an amateur can create a beautiful bathroom design.

However, the lay person really isn't qualified to tackle technical aspects, such as plumbing and electricity. Although your general contractor may be able to advise you on these areas, you could choose to put the whole design in the hands of an expert rather than do it yourself.

five types of designer

1 • Architect: Trained in structural design, most will usually take on only major works, such as the design or re-modeling of a whole house.
2 • Interior architect: Combines structural expertise with an interior design service.
3 • Interior designer: Focuses on the inside of a home, rather than the external structure. May be able to tackle straightforward structural changes.
4 • Interior decorator: Offers a service of "superficial" decorating, rather than technical or structural alterations.
5 • Bathroom designer: Employed by a bathroom showroom, a bathroom designer demonstrates how the retailer's products can be used to create a dream bathroom. Some may be solely design-led, whereas others may be more sales-led, so be sure you understand their motivation.

who does what?

Be sure you decide with your designer where responsibility lies. Who will manage the project? Who will choose and hire the contractors? Who will be in charge of final decoration? There are many different levels of design service, so check exactly what you will be paying for. Make sure there's a contract and that you fully understand it.

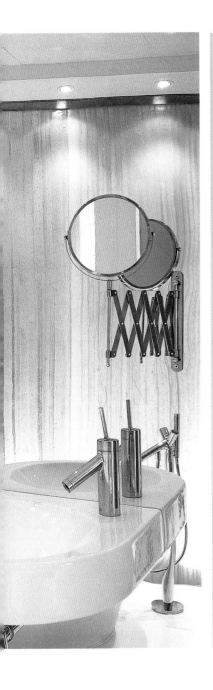

bathroom contractors

Unless you're an expert at home improvement and have the right qualifications to do all the work yourself, you'll be calling on the services of professionals to help you complete your bathroom project.

Just think of all the different elements in a bathroom. You (or your designer) may need to hire a whole team of workers, including a plumber, plasterer, tiler, electrician, and painter. But often you'll hire just one person, a general contractor. He (or she) will be capable of doing the heavy work, and even the more specialized jobs like plastering or tiling, but may sub-contract the plumbing and electrical jobs to other professionals. This will save you the responsibility of doing more hiring, and your main contractor will oversee their work and pay them for it.

Of course, finding a reliable and talented contractor is never easy. You'll hear plenty of horror stories about unreliable and dishonest operators.

Picking a name at random out of the phone book is risky, so to give yourself the best chance of getting it right:

• Ask friends and neighbors for recommendations.

• Get estimates from at least three tradespeople.

• Make sure that your contractor is a member of the relevant professional group and is fully qualified.

• Ask any potential contractors for references—and make sure that you check them.

• Make sure your contractor carries insurance—for personal injury, for injury the work may cause to others, and for damage to goods or property.

• Get a written contract that includes a schedule of payments (with a 5% fee to be held back until you're satisfied with the work) and penalty clauses in case of late completion.

• Check whether the work will be guaranteed or not.

plumbing

Water supply and drainage, faucets and showers, water-based heating systems—these are all the remit of the plumber. This specialized tradesperson is invaluable in bathroom installations, not least because he or she can bring practical experience to the project, as well as technical know-how.

what a plumber can do for you

• Rough plumbing: Investigating and upgrading the below-floor or wall-buried pipework; installing pipes to fit the layout of the new bathroom
• Water pressure: Measuring your water pressure, so you know what faucets and shower will be suitable; boosting the water pressure if necessary
• Heating: Upgrading your hot water and heating systems, if necessary; advising on (and installing) a new heating appliance for the bathroom
• Installation: Of the toilet, shower, faucets, and sink, connecting the hot and cold feeds, and connecting the drainage pipes to the waste pipes
• Specifying: Buying basic bathroom fixtures and fittings at reduced prices from trade suppliers

Make sure you check that your plumber is fully qualified for all aspects of the work (including installing a water heater, for example). Different aspects of plumbing are governed by health and safety or building codes, particularly regarding water supply and sanitation, and you need to be assured that these are being correctly followed.

9
the water heater

There's a great range of water heaters. Most run on either gas or electricity, but they vary in their capacity and in the way they operate; some store hot water, some heat up cold water instantly on demand and thus save energy. In recent decades solar-powered water heaters have become more common.

It's important you understand what type of system you have so you can make decisions regarding the products you'll install in your bathroom. For example, there's no point fitting a big bathtub if your water heater can't supply sufficient hot water to fill it. And if you want to be able to run two showers at the same time, you'll need to have a high-pressure, high-capacity system.

Ask your plumber for advice on what your current system is capable of, and consider whether you need to change or upgrade your system to achieve your dream bathroom.

10
electricity— and water

Water and electricity are a dangerous mix, which is why there are so many regulations governing such matters as the use of electrical appliances, voltage limits, and types of electrical outlet permitted in wet areas. However, regulations vary greatly between countries, from the types of switches and outlets allowed (if at all) in the room to the qualifications needed (if any) before someone can tackle electrical work in bathrooms.

what an electrician can do for you

• Lighting: Your electrician should be able to advise on the types of light fixtures you need, such as waterproof, water-resistant, or low-voltage, and will wire up the system safely

• Switches and outlets: Ask for guidance on the positioning of outlets and switches. Let him know exactly what you wish to use the outlets for—electric shaver, toothbrush, hairdryer, etc., so he can ensure they meet all safety requirements

• Electrically operated plumbing: Pump systems (for supplying or draining water) work by electricity, and also water is heated electrically in some water heaters. Your plumber may be trained to complete the installation; otherwise it's best to turn to an electrician

• Ventilation: It's essential—and in some countries, a window in the bathroom is required by law. Ducted systems suck steam and odors outside, keeping the air fresh and reducing moisture in the bathroom. Ventilation often works in conjunction with the lighting, activated when the light is switched on, but running for another 15–20 minutes after the light is extinguished

best-laid plans

11

Whether you're doing everything yourself or calling in contractors, you'll need plans to refer to while you renovate. Mistakes occur when ideas are left vague, so creating a drawing will ensure that the redesign is kept on track.

floor plan

• Make yourself a rough pencil sketch of the shape of the room, as seen from a bird's-eye view.

• Measure and mark down the length of every wall, and section of wall. Also measure the height of the room and note this alongside the sketch.

• Measure the width and height of windows and doors and note where they start and finish. Mark those on the drawing, too. Add details such as the swing of the door.

• Mark plumbing outlets such as the waste pipe, and any major or permanent fixtures such as a water heater, or any housing for pipes.

• Now transfer this rough sketch to a piece of graph paper, drawing it accurately to scale.

You could also sketch each elevation (i.e., what a wall looks like as you face it) to show heights, but the basic bird's-eye-view floor plan is normally enough to design a layout.

layout

Take careful note of the measurements of the bathtub, toilet, sink, vanity units, and other fixtures you want to include in your bathroom. Draw them to the same scale as the floor plan and cut them out. Now position them on your plan to see what will fit, and make sure you consider circulation space around each piece, and the height they reach.

mood board

To help you decide on the look you want (or to help your interior designer know your tastes), collect samples of tiles, paint charts, fabric swatches, and lots of clippings from magazines and brochures. Glue them in place on cardboard to give a visual overview of the general "mood" you want in your finished bathroom.

structural alterations 12

With your floor plan in front of you, strewn with cut-out pieces of paper that you're trying to arrange into a sensible layout, you may despair of the size or shape of the bathroom. And standing in a dark and dingy space, with a low, oppressive ceiling and awkwardly positioned fixtures, you may think it can never be a light and welcoming room.

It is possible to alter the shell of the room and to change the structure to your advantage. But are you prepared for extra expense and upheaval? Bear in mind, too, there may be delays while you wait for permission to make the changes (in some cases, structural alterations are governed by local building codes, and you need approval before you can start—check with your designer, contractor, or local planning office).

three good reasons for structural alterations

1 to create more physical space

Demolishing walls to borrow space from a neighboring room and removing bulky obstacles such as cupboards will enlarge the bathroom, giving you more room to fit in everything you want.

2 to enhance the sense of space

Raising or lowering a ceiling or floor, resizing windows, or adding a skylight are all ways of improving the space you have. Concealing pipes, bringing in more natural light, and creating better proportions will do wonders for a small bathroom, too (see 13).

3 to increase the flexibility of design

Strengthening the walls allows you to wall-mount fixtures, while strengthening the floor will enable the joists to support a cast-iron tub. Simply by repositioning the waste pipe, moving the door, or even changing the way it swings, you open up new layout possibilities.

bijou bathrooms 13

If allowed to change only one thing about their bathroom, most people would ask for a bigger space. But, unfortunately, since it's not always possible to wave a magic wand and make the walls move outward, the majority learn to live with the tight dimensions of the room.

All is not lost, though, for with careful planning and judicious selection of fixtures, you can create a small bathroom that displays a regard for aesthetic factors, maximizes every inch of space, and even fools the eye into thinking the closed-in walls are not so close after all.

five solutions for small bathrooms

1 • Cutting it fine: Having realized that small bathrooms are a big problem, many companies are now offering space-saving solutions. Look for shortened or tapered bathtubs, short-projection sinks, and off-set toilets, as well as reduced-depth cabinets.

2 • Hanging it all: The eye looks at the floor space and judges the size of the room accordingly, so if you mount your sink, toilet, (see 58), and furniture on the wall, you'll immediately create the impression of more space in the room.

3 • Doubling up: Fit two items into one space—for example, a bath-shower combination, furniture that doubles as a sink support, or a laundry basket that's also a seat.

4 • On reflection: Mirrors are an excellent means of visually expanding a space. A wall-to-wall mirror will appear to double the size of the room, and even a small mirror can be positioned to bounce light around the bathroom.

5 • Light relief: Choose light colors to make surfaces recede, such as white-tiled walls, beige stone flooring, and translucent green glass screens.

big bathrooms

In some ways, big bathrooms are as hard to design as small ones. The more flexibility you have, the more difficult it can be.

three common mistakes in designing big bathrooms

1 • Wall-hugging: In small bathrooms, most products will butt up against walls. In big bathrooms they don't have to—and in fact, it looks wrong if all the fixtures seem to shrink away from the center of the room and hug the perimeter.

2 • Overloading: You may have room for a toilet, bidet, two-person bathtub, steam cabinet, twin sinks, built-in furniture—but you don't have to have it all. There's no formula for the perfect bathroom, so choose only those pieces you will actually use.

3 • Over-styling: Don't think that big has to mean grand. You can keep your bathroom simple without it seeming empty, and you don't have to fill it with paraphernalia or make it look too busy.

three good ideas for big bathrooms

1 • Focusing: Consider using a big, freestanding bathtub as a focal point in the room. It doesn't have to be slap-bang in the middle: Use it to draw your eye through the room or toward one corner.

2 • Zoning: Use partitions, changes in floor height, and different colors/materials to define zones. For example, hide the toilet behind a glass-block wall, and separate wet areas from dry areas with different floor coverings.

3 • Expanding: Don't expand the area, but expand the use of the bathroom. Can you use a section as a walk-in closet, or create a comfortable sitting area in one corner where you can pamper yourself?

en-suite bathrooms

Adjacent to the bedroom, the en-suite, or connecting bath has a specialized and personal nature. Besides thinking about the generalities encountered in any bathroom renovation, consider the design issues peculiar to the en-suite bath.

• Free flowing: Whereas a family bathroom opens off a hallway, an en-suite bath is an extension of a bedroom. For that reason, design coherence between the two rooms, such as a similar color scheme, textures, or materials in both, is very important.

• Personal taste: Casual visitors won't usually see your en-suite bathroom. This means that you can really make it a design to please you—not a showpiece for guests. View it as a chance to explore your own ideas and experiment a little with design.

• Privacy: How open or how private your private bath is depends on you (and the person you may share the bedroom with). If you don't close the door, do you even need one?

finding the space

Creating an en-suite bathroom where none exists isn't always simple, but it's worth the effort for the convenience it brings. It's also likely to raise the saleability of your property, as a private bath is often rated a necessity, rather than a luxury. Here are three ways you might find the space:

1 Borrowing: If there's space to spare in the room next door, consider borrowing some (or all) of it for this bathroom.

2 Partitioning: If your bedroom is large enough, you can partition off a section of the room to create a bathroom.

3 Adapting: Even a closet, a hallway, or a landing can be` turned into a shower room, with some clever design work and professional help.

open-plan bathrooms

A relatively new trend, but one that's attracting growing interest, is the open-plan bathroom. A bolder, braver version of the en-suite bath, this is a bathroom within a bedroom—with no walls for privacy. Its extremely open nature means it's not suitable for all lifestyles and tastes, so it may be worth building flexibility into the design, allowing it to be "walled away" if your situation changes.

three practical aspects to consider

1 • Disturbance: If you share your bedroom with a partner, make sure you're both on the same timetable. If one gets up earlier or goes to bed later than the other, the person sleeping will be disturbed by the noise of water running, by lights being switched on, and by general bustle in the open-plan bathroom.

2 • Privacy: In a family house, you may want to put a lock on the bedroom door so you can bathe and use the toilet without fear of interruption. And on the subject of the toilet, no matter how close you are to your partner, there are probably some things you just don't want to share! So consider tucking the toilet behind a screen or creating a separate area to house it.

3 • Ventilation: There's a lot of fabric in a bedroom—curtains, linens, and sometimes carpeting, too. Unless you want to risk your clothes getting damp or your shower curtain's growing moldy, good ventilation is essential to prevent condensation.

17 the family bathroom

The typical family bathroom has multiple roles to play: a fun-filled water park for young kids, a beauty parlor or grooming zone for teenagers, a quiet retreat for Mom or Dad. . . . Its main purpose is, of course, to house essential washing facilities (toilet, bathtub, shower, and sink).

Because the family bathroom is used by a variety of people ranging in age and size, with different needs and tastes, the design shouldn't be too radical or geared too much toward either adults or children. Make moderation, practicality, and flexibility your watchwords.

moderation
• Standard fixtures in white or cream are inoffensive and will stand the test of time.

• If sinks and toilets are too high, the children will struggle to reach them; if they're too low you'll have to stoop uncomfortably.

practicality
• With kids around, things are sure to get dropped and spilled, and water will certainly be splashed around, so make sure your floor and wall coverings can cope.

• It's amazing how much grime teenagers bring into the house—have you seen a bathtub after a football game? Quick-clean surfaces will make life much easier.

flexibility
• If toys for children's bathtime clutter the room, make sure there's plenty of storage where you can bundle them away before your relaxing soak in the tub. You want to be able to switch from mayhem to calm with minimum effort.

• Lines forming outside a family bathroom in the morning are not unusual. Consider creating a separate half-bath or providing a sink in a teenager's bedroom, to decrease the strain on the family bathroom.

18

the children's bathroom

If your child is lucky enough to have a dedicated bathroom, you can decorate it with kids-only in mind. But even so, remember that little ones don't stay little—allow some leeway for the bathroom to adapt as children grow up.

three essential elements of children's bathrooms

1 practicality

• Set the toilet and sink low (or with a small step in front) so children can reach easily.
• Set the bathtub into a step so the sides are low enough for little ones to climb in and out.
• Make sure all surfaces are waterproof, and durable enough to withstand any hard knocks.

2 fun

• Kids love color, so wave goodbye to any thoughts of neutrals. Consider bright waterproof paint, a border of tiles in zesty shades, or even colorful stickers to jazz up plain white tiles or fixtures.
• Buy a toy chest that doubles as a seat, use decorated or shaped mirrors that are angled downward, and add fun doorknobs, drawer handles, and clothes hooks.
• Create a theme around a cartoon character, using lots of accessories and logos to set the scene.

3 safety

• Hot water is a big danger, so make sure the faucets and shower have anti-scald devices and thermostatic controls are set to low temperatures.
• Never leave a small child unattended in the bath in case of drowning.
• Choose a non-slip, soft-underfoot floor covering, like cork or cushioned vinyl. Add a rubber bathmat so children don't slip in the tub.
• Make sure there's no lock on the door so children can't get locked in.

the personal sanctuary

If you need a place to rest and unwind, a retreat from the demands of everyday living, establish the bathroom as your private sanctuary. No longer simply a room for cleansing the body, the bathroom can also detoxify the mind.

A personal sanctuary is as individual as its creator. For some, deep-pile towels, hydro-massage showers, and a wealth of expensive scrubs and soaps are essential. Others prefer a more ascetic, pared-down experience. But whether you opt for high-maintenance heaven or the simplest haven, there are three things you can't do without:

1 • A comfortable bathtub: It doesn't have to be enormous or boast whirlpool jets—all you need is a tub that will cradle your body as you lie back and relax.

2 • Adjustable lighting: If you have lights on dimmers, you can turn them down to a comfortable glow. Failing that, switch off all the lights and bathe by candlelight.

3 • A lock on the door: Make sure you can't be interrupted as you soak away your stress!

20 the home spa

Even without a masseuse on hand, you can turn your bathroom into a private spa. Be inspired by health clubs to create a hydro-therapy zone that will invigorate or relax, as your mood takes you.

Whirlpool or spa baths, steam cabinets, and multi-jet showers all offer a range of multi-sensory therapeutic benefits. These include

• Hydro-massage: Varying spray patterns, pulses of water, and bubbling air have a range of positive effects, including improving circulation, relaxing muscles, and easing joints.
• Chromotherapy: Top-of-the-range bathtubs and shower stalls boast light therapy, creating positive psychological effects with colored lighting (for example, red to stimulate, yellow for happiness, orange to revitalize, and green for relaxation).
• Aromatherapy: Some steam cabinets include infusers to waft the scent of aromatic oils or herbs into the cabinet (otherwise, you can add essential oils to a burner by the side of the bath).

21 the wet room

A wet room—a bathroom with a shower but no shower base—is at the cutting edge of bathroom design. The water from the shower cascades onto the floor, where a drainage system channels it away. Often, the water is allowed to splash freely, as there's no shower enclosure; however, in some cases, a screen or wall is erected to protect other areas of the bathroom.

Although a wet room looks simple, creating a leak-proof room is very complex. Firstly, the whole structure of the room must be stable: wooden joists may need to be stabilized so they don't flex. For this reason, wet rooms suit the first floor or basement, rather than an upper floor. The entire room will need to be tanked (waterproofed), usually with a layer of bitumen, fiberglass, or lead. On top of this is laid the watertight floor- and wall-covering, such as stone or ceramic tiles, and the grout must be totally waterproof—an epoxy-resin mixture, for example.

spray on

The showering system in your wet room could be a ceiling-mounted showerhead, a wall-mounted handset, or even a multi-jet shower panel. And if you have enough space, you can position the shower away from the wall and install a freestanding central column.

your style dare you defy definition? 22

You might not have actually put a name to the style you prefer, or you may not think your taste can be neatly pigeonholed into a particular category, but it's likely that your bathroom will veer toward one of the following five styles.

1 clinical

Imagine a laboratory-like space: Hygienic, wipe-clean surfaces in stainless steel, polished chrome and high-gloss white acrylic, expanses of white tiles, accents of frosty green glass, streamlined storage. Although somewhat cold and hard in appearance, the clinical bathroom is a minimalist's heaven.

2 organic

A back-to-nature feel, where glaring white is banished in favor of soft cream. Wood and stone, with prominent grain and rough texture, are an integral part of the design, whether in the form of a sink, flooring, or accessories. Tiles in neutral colors and with pitted surfaces carry a raw feel. Add a jungle of plants for bathroom wilderness.

3 classic

Elegantly traditional: gold-colored faucets with ceramic handles and flared spouts, decorative tiles in deeper tones, a claw-foot bathtub. A dark wood vanity unit with a Carrara marble surround adds rich appeal. The window is dressed with curtains or draperies.

4 colorful

The bolder, the better: If you're brave enough, choose colored fixtures and team them with complementary shades of paint on the walls and bright linoleum flooring. Or opt for plain white fixtures, and choose a single accent color, going crazy with bright mosaic tiles, rich fluffy towels, and patterned roller shades.

5 eclectic

A mix-and-match approach, in which the traditional is confidently combined with the contemporary, and the bold and bright are placed alongside naturals and neutrals. Styled with flair, it doesn't look haphazard, but is balanced to create a warm and user-friendly bathroom.

contemporary 23

The word "minimalist" is much over-used in describing clean-lined, contemporary homes, but few really embrace the absolute spirit of minimalism. The in-vogue bathroom is more likely to follow a path of comfortable minimalism that balances simplicity and pared-down lines with the practicalities of everyday family life.

five typical materials

1 • Glass: Acid-etched or sandblasted, frosted glass has an attractive icy appearance. Tinging it with green, blue, or gray will add a gentle hint of color to the design.

2 • Ceramic: White ceramic fixtures follow strictly simple geometry (squares and circles are both popular), while white ceramic tiles, in brick shapes or squares, offer subtle texture for interest. Ceramic mosaics in watery colors are often used for shower areas.

3 • Stone: Slate flooring brings a rougher, organic feel underfoot; expanses of pale, honed limestone denote simplicity.

4 • Metal: Shower controls and faucets are plated in silvery chrome, stainless steel, or aluminum, and the same polished or matte metals are used as accents elsewhere.

5 • Wood: Basins, shelves, and accessories in tropical hardwoods such as wenge or iroko (preferably from sustainable resources) or in fashionable plywood are teamed with harder materials for interesting contrast.

five typical products

1 • Bathtubs and showers: High-tech spa products including steam cabinets, whirlpool tubs, and hydro-massage showers

2 • Toilet: wall-mounted toilet, with the cistern concealed and a discreet push-button flush

3 • Radiator: Ladder-style radiators and towel warmers, wall-hung to conserve space

4 • Furniture: Simple vanity unit in chunky wood, often just a shelf cantilevered from the wall, with double sinks inset or mounted on top

5 • Fittings: Single-lever faucets, wall-mounted to conceal all the pipework

traditional

Typically Colonial, Victorian, or Art Deco in style, the traditionally styled bathroom exudes comfort and warmth. Colors are deeper and materials softer (even fabric makes an appearance), and decorative details have no purpose other than to please the eye.

five typical materials

1 • Glass: Traditional glass tends to be crystal clear or etched with patterns for both decoration and privacy.

2 • Ceramic: Fixtures are off-white and molded with rims, lips, and decorative plinths. Tiles are colored in deep, glossy hues or printed with border designs and other motifs.

3 • Stone: Marble and speckled granite add robust and classical notes to the room; used not only on walls and floors but also for bath and sink surrounds.

4 • Metal: Shower and faucets are plated in warm, burnished metals, such as brass, or brass alloyed with nickel or pewter.

5 • Wood: Furniture is finished with rich mahogany and cherry wood veneers, and elaborate carving adds an opulent note.

five typical products

1 • Bathtubs and showers: Enameled, cast-iron bathtubs, the exterior painted in chalky shades, perch on claw-foot legs; the shower features a ceramic handle.

2 • Toilet: The wooden-seated toilet stands like an elegant throne, with a visible cistern and pull-chain flush.

3 • Radiator: A cast-iron column radiator in pewter or painted finish stands underneath the window.

4 • Furniture: Deep floor-standing vanity units with molded panels and marble tops hold inset oval sinks.

5 • Fittings: Top-mounted pillar faucets and bridge faucets display fluted spouts and chunky cross handles or ceramic levers.

project management

Any project, whether it's a bathroom renovation or a business endeavor, needs a manager. This person has an overview of the whole work, is a central point of contact for all involved, and really understands "the big picture." The manager can be hands-on or can choose to delegate tasks appropriately and check results to make sure that the jobs have been completed to satisfaction. He or she bears ultimate responsibility for the success of the project.

should I project manage?

You need to decide whether you will be project manager on your own bathroom refurbishment. Be realistic:

• Do you have the time? If it's a major job, you'll need to be around to oversee the work or be there to deal with problems when they crop up.

• Do you have the skills? You'll need to liaise with the professional tilers, plumbers, etc.—can you explain to them what you need them to do?

• Can you afford to hire anyone else? Although it's unlikely you'll be hiring someone who is simply a project manager (unless you're building or revamping a whole house), you could put the responsibility of project management on your interior designer, architect, or even a general contractor who is carrying out the renovation work.

project management involves controlling

• Costs: Keep the project on budget by ensuring that the right products—and the correct amounts—are bought. If the unexpected occurs, be prepared to use some of your contingency fund, but see if there's another solution apart from pouring money in.

• Schedule: Make sure not only that work is completed on time but also that all the products arrive on time—this is basic supply-chain management. You have to make sure that the tiles you ordered 4 weeks ago will arrive when your tiler needs them.

• Quality: Check the work as each stage is being completed. Look at the pipes before they're covered over; check the finish on the plastered walls. Make sure you're happy with one job before another begins.

step-by-step

Your head may be spinning with ideas; you're unsure where to start or how to structure the renovation project. It helps to make a list of everything you have to do and then draft a timeline, so you know your priorities.

ten-point checklist

1 • Begin your research: Get inspiration from showrooms and catalogs. Ask lots of questions, visit web forums, read articles. You can spend months doing this while you save up your money.

2 • Make lists: Note your likes and dislikes, what you want to include (or avoid) in your new bathroom; make a wish list of your dream items.

3 • Set a budget: Consider how much money you're willing to spend on the bathroom; whittle your wish list down to your "must-haves" and start collecting information on prices of products; get labor estimates from possible contractors.

4 • Select a contractor or contractors: Having negotiated fees and checked references, have in-depth discussions with your chosen contractor about availability, time schedule, and responsibilities.

5 • Draw up plans: Sketch a floor plan to scale, and make a final decision about the products that you want. Involve your contractor in the technical aspects.

6 • Order products: Order all the tiles, faucets, the bathtub, sinks, etc., and check if other materials are needed (e.g., will your tiler supply the grout?). Find out the lead times for each product. (If you're ordering European goods, bear in mind that some factories there shut for a month in the summer.)

7 • Sign a contract: Now that you and your contractor know the timings, products, and every detail, negotiate a final fee and agree a contract.

8 • Start renovating: Your contractor (or you) can now commence the operation by gutting the original bathroom.

9 • Oversee the project: Even if you're not project managing, it's worth sticking your head into the bathroom occasionally to see how work is progressing. Aim to avert problems before they happen or solve them as they arise.

10 • Final details: Check the bathroom thoroughly, with your contractor and alone. Present the contractor with a list of any necessary adjustments (e.g., straighten shelf, replace chipped tiles), and don't pay the balance until your bathroom is totally finished and you are completely happy with it.

part two

getting down to the detail

it's bathtime

The bathtub is usually the single largest element of a bathroom, and its size alone makes it a focal point. But add good looks, design innovation, and ergonomic styling to its monolithic bulk, and you'll have a centerpiece you can be proud of.

testing, testing

Don't be embarrassed about climbing into the tub in the showroom and sitting up and lying back in it. Does it offer good support for your neck, back, and arms? Is it both long enough and wide enough? Above all, is it comfortable?

inside out

Besides actually testing the bathtub to check its comfort, make a point of looking at the specifications in the brochure, which detail the internal dimensions as well as external ones. Compare different models, and try to find the one with the most internal space.

the impact of color

For the past few years, simple white has been the favored color for tubs. Now, however, focal-point tubs come in all shades, from bright-hued composites to translucent glass. Don't be frightened of opting for color, but temper it with some white fixtures.

twice as nice

Shared bathing won't be romantic and relaxing unless it's comfortable. Look for a double-ended bath that slopes gently at both ends (you can both lean back), with a central drain (so no one sits on the plug!), and no pre-drilled faucet holes at one end (you can install faucets centrally).

outsiders

With the exception of certain tubs, such as claw-foots, most bathtubs require aprons or panels to give them a finished appearance. Consider how your bath will look when installed. Do you want to box it in and tile the surround, or add acrylic side and end panels to match? You can even find stylish patterned glass or metal vanity surrounds.

28 material matters

Glass, wood, stone, and even stainless steel tubs are now available, but the three most common materials are acrylic, cast iron, and pressed steel.

acrylic

Available in numerous colors (though white is the current trend), acrylic also gives the greatest variety in terms of shape and size. Look for acrylic composites, which are stronger and won't flex so much, and double-skinned acrylics for greater heat insulation.

advantages

- Can be molded into complex shapes.
- Is lightweight.
- Is super-smooth and non-porous.
- Is warm to the touch.
- Won't chip.

disadvantages

- Cheaper acrylics are flimsy and will flex.
- Needs strengthening with glass fiber or wooden supports.
- Thin acrylics aren't very heat insulating.
- May scratch and stain.

cast iron

Traditional style cast iron bathtubs come with a vitreous enamel interior, and the exterior comes ready-painted, or primed for your own color choice. Look at the beautiful uneven surface of the enamel glaze inside a cast-iron tub; it suggests a unique and timeless beauty that more modern materials can't capture.

advantages

- Offers excellent heat insulation (once the material has warmed up).
- Is durable and stable.
- Exterior can be color-matched to your décor.
- Is scratch-resistant.

disadvantages

- Is extremely heavy.
- Is limited in shape and size due to weight and rigidity.
- Enamel may chip.

pressed steel

For the best of both worlds, look at enameled pressed steel; it's an excellent compromise between the lightweight malleability of acrylic and the solidity of cast iron. Look for tubs with thicker layers of steel for greater strength and better heat insulation.

advantages

- Is relatively strong and durable.
- Offers choice of shapes.
- Is scratch resistant.
- Is lightweight.
- Is cost-effective.

disadvantages

- Thinner layers of steel are not very heat-insulating.
- Enamel may chip.

shapes 29

It's important to consider both the external and internal shape of a bathtub. The external shape will influence where you locate the tub in your bathroom and what you can place alongside it, while the internal shape will have more bearing on your comfort and how easy (or difficult) it will be to clean the bath.

rectangle

The straight sides and right angles of the boxy shape enable the bath to be positioned flush with a wall or tight into a corner, while the rounded internal angles cradle the body better and are easy to clean.

oval

An oval exterior is usually found on a freestanding tub, such as a claw-foot, which is ideal for central placement in the bathroom. The soft angles and the rounded interior make it comfortable to sit or lie in.

round

Although the external shape is smooth and ergonomic, circular tubs are bulky and demand a big bathroom. The internal shape makes it easier to sit up than to lie down, unless it's molded to hold one or two bodies.

corner

Quadrant-shaped corner bathtubs present a soft curve to the room, but do take up a lot of space. The internal shape is sometimes a little awkward, so look for models specially contoured to the body.

offset or tapered

An offset corner tub or tapered rectangle give the benefits of those common shapes, but in a more space-saving form.

small and snug

30

Although an average rectangular bathtub measures about 60 x 32 inches, if your bathroom suffers from space restrictions, even this standard size can be a problem.

• Length: Several manufacturers offer space-saving baths starting from 4 feet long in a variety of styles and sizes.
• Width: Look for baths that are 30 to 32 inches wide, but bear in mind the tight internal dimensions of anything narrower.

To make sure your bathing experience in a small bathtub is as comfortable as possible, look for tapered or offset styles (the narrower end will be the foot end), deep tubs (if you can't lie flat, at least the water will still cover you), and straight internal sides (you lose a lot of space if the bath slopes inward).

the bigger, the better?

31

If you're blessed with a large bathroom, surely it makes sense to fill the space with a capacious bathtub? But before you take the plunge and opt for a 6 foot monolith, weigh the potential drawbacks against the obvious luxurious benefits.

how long will it take to fill the tub?

Depending on the water pressure (and the flow rate your bathtub faucet allows), it could take 15 minutes or more to fill the tub to a reasonable level.

how much hot water?

If you have a boiler, check the hot water storage capacity. You may find your tank runs dry before your bathtub is even half full.

how much will it cost?

This consideration is not just the cost of the tub itself (although big tubs do tend to be expensive), but the amount of water it uses and the amount of energy needed to heat that water. It's not the most environmentally friendly, or cost-conscious option.

modern bathtubs

Sleek lines and architectural geometry distinguish the contemporary bathtub. But that's where the generalizations end. It can't be categorized by a single material, color, style, or size. And ongoing product development and technological advances have allowed the modern bathtub to break free of its past limitations.

big and boxy

Defined by high, straight sides and sharp angles, these freestanding giants are made possible by the strength and stability of composite materials that mix stone with resin, or even acrylic with more robust components.

pillow talk

In addition to interiors contoured to cocoon your body, you'll find integrated bath pillows or removable backrests. Many contemporary tubs are designed to offer a high degree of internal comfort.

bottoms up

A modern variation on the claw-foot style sees this oval tub raised off the ground on a wooden platform or plinth or in a tubular steel cradle. The added height and mix of materials add a new dimension to the design.

sailing away

Boat-building technology comes into play in the construction of waterproof tubs made from tropical hardwoods (see 23) or marine ply. They require maintenance to remain watertight, but are worth it for the stunning organic centerpiece they create.

fill 'er up

A faucet is the usual means of filling a bathtub. However, a neat contemporary option is a bath filler actually inside the tub, commonly integrated into the overflow. It delivers a strong stream of water to quickly fill the tub and takes away the problem of where to site the faucet.

33 traditional bathtubs

With its classical elegance, the claw-foot bathtub continues to hold its place at the heart of the traditional bathroom, and in recent years, it has been borrowed by the modernists to form a centerpiece in the contemporary bathroom, too.

three types of traditional tub

1 • Original: With ornate claw feet, enameled interior, and painted exterior. You can get these cast-iron antiques from salvage yards and specialized dealers.

2 • Reproduction: Identical in style to the original, these are newly made and readily available. Some use lighter materials, such as acrylic composites (see 28).

3 • Updated: Drawing on the lines of the classic claw-foot, the modern version substitutes tubular steel legs, or even a plinth for the claw feet (see 32).

Some claw-foot tubs have a squared-off end, so the tub can be placed against a wall or in a corner, but most are oval-shaped freestanding pieces. This means that the waste pipe and hot- and cold-water feeds will be visible where they exit and enter the bath. The pipes to the tub will need to run below the floor, and some structural work may be required, depending on the joists and subfloor. You may even need to raise the height of the floor or create a platform for the bathtub to stand on (see 12).

Other traditional bathtub forms are the slipper style and the bateau tub. A slipper bath has one end raised higher than the other, forming a shape that resembles an arched shoe—hence its name. The bateau takes its title from the French word for boat, and is a high-sided, flat-bottomed tub, often in burnished, hand-beaten copper.

34

spa and whirlpool baths—time to pamper yourself

Whirlpool and spa baths are the ultimate luxury in the bathroom, creating a private pampering zone where you can sink into bubbling water, blissfully while away the hours, and wave away your bodily aches (see 19 and 20).

same difference?

The terms "spa" and "whirlpool" are sometimes used synonymously, but the two methods of hydro-massage are actually very different.

• Spa bath: Holes in the base of the bath bubble air upward for a soft, fizzy feeling. Spa baths commonly have 150–200 microjets for complete body coverage.

• Whirlpool bath: Water is sucked inward and injected back into the bath with force. It's a much stronger effect than a spa, and it's usual to have only 6–12 jets, positioned around the sides of the bath to target specific areas such as neck, back, and feet.

• Spa-whirlpool combos: Some baths combine spa jets with whirlpool jets for a dual-action massage. They can be used simultaneously or independently.

medical miracles?

The health benefits of hydro-massage are widely recognized: improved blood circulation, stimulated lymphatic drainage, increased oxygenation to the skin, and relaxed muscles. It's ideal if you're feeling tense and aching, and is also believed to help lessen the pain of arthritis and rheumatism. The soothing psychological effects of a relaxing massage should not be underestimated either.

stay safe and sound

Hygiene is a vital consideration with home spa systems. Stagnant water lingering in the pipework can be a breeding ground for bacteria. Look for the following features:

• Inclined pipes: These will facilitate water drainage.

• Closed jets: If the bath is in use without the whirlpool, the jets are sealed to prevent soap and sediment from entering.

• Air drying: Warm air is blown through the pipes after use to ensure that they are totally dry.

• Disinfection system: Cleaning fluids are released into the pipes to ensure that bacteria can't linger.

• UV light system: This sanitizes the pipes by destroying bacteria.

careful!

With regard to safety, look for jets that have an automatic cut-off if they become blocked (for example, by your hair). Bear in mind, too, that low-voltage electricity is involved, as both the pump and touch-button controls are electrically operated. Always ask a qualified professional to install whatever system you choose.

comfort zone

Your massage bath needs to be a totally relaxing experience, so look for a comfortable internal shape, including armrests, footrests, and soft head and neck cushions. Also, consider noise levels: if the system is too loud, you won't be able to relax. Ask to hear a model tested in the showroom, or choose a brand that boasts whisper-quiet operation.

extra features

The top models are packed with extra features including integrated radios and CD players, soothing soundtracks (rainforest effects, for example), underwater lights, chromotherapy settings, and even ultrasound massage.

grand plans or small spaces

If your immediate thought is that you can't fit a spa or whirlpool tub into your modest-sized bathroom, don't despair. They really do come in all shapes and sizes. From large corner models or freestanding round tubs for two or more people to shorter, narrow, sit-up tubs for small bathrooms.

over-tub showers

If you lack the space for a shower enclosure in addition to a bathtub, an over-bath shower offers an ideal solution. And even if your bathroom does boast a separate shower enclosure, a secondary shower above the tub will be useful for rinsing off soap and when cleaning the bathtub.

You can create your own over-bath shower very simply, with a standard bathtub. A basic shower attachment can be retrofitted with surprising ease, but if you are totally renovating the bathroom, then plan for a fixed showerhead above, or a wall-mounted shower attachment on a glide rail.

Some companies offer tubs specifically designed for over-bath showers. They are modified to allow for more comfortable showering and offer a variety of useful benefits.

space to maneuver

Special bath-shower tubs bulge outward at one end, to create a circular or square area that acts as a generous showering space. You may have as much as 8 inches extra elbow room at the shower end.

grip, not slip

Specialized bathtubs incorporate a textured surface at the showering end to give your feet some traction, so you don't have to use a rubber mat to stop yourself from slipping.

screening program

Tubs with a rounded showering end come with their own custom-fitted, curved glass screens to keep splashes inside. If you are simply modifying a standard straight-sided tub, though, it won't be a problem to fit a straight glass panel (see 36).

obstacle course

Do think about where you are positioning faucets, soap dishes, and storage racks in relation to the showering area. You don't want them where you'll bang your knees and elbows—but you will want your toiletries within easy reach.

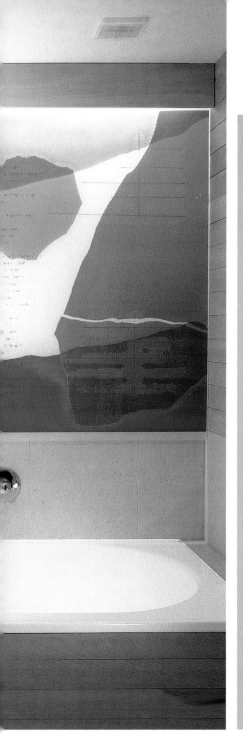

bathtub screens

If you're showering over the bath, you usually need a means of keeping the water within the bounds of the tub. With a hand-held attachment that you use simply for rinsing soapsuds off yourself and the tub, you could just hold the showerhead low and direct it carefully—and hope for the best! Splashes are inevitable, but they can be limited.

For a ceiling-mounted shower or a shower on a glide rail, you'll definitely need effective protection to stop your bathroom floor from flooding. You could go for the cheap and easy option of a shower curtain—but are you prepared to clean it frequently and to replace it regularly? A better option is a solid screen or panel made of tempered or safety glass.

fixed screen

This is an immobile screen sealed at the bottom and side. It is more difficult to access the bathtub, the faucets, and the inside of the screen for cleaning, but it is less likely to leak.

swing or pivot

Hinged at the side, and with a rubber seal at the bottom, a swing or pivot screen gives easier access to the bathtub, but if it's not fitted properly, or as the rubber deteriorates, it may leak.

folding screen

When not in use, the best versions fold flat against the wall for total access to the bathtub. However, if the wall is out-of-true, they may not stay in place, and as with a swing screen, leakage can occur.

sliding

You can recess a bath into an alcove and create a fully enclosed showering area with a sliding screen (see 43).

it's curtains?

Shower curtains have a reputation for turning smelly and damp, harboring unsightly and unhealthy mold and mildew, and wrapping wetly around you while you are showering. However, a new generation of heavy-duty plastic curtains are weighty enough not to flap around, and some even have integrated mold-inhibitors.

37

showering with style

5 ideas

There's more to choosing a shower than simply picking the one that you think looks good. You must do your homework first and consider practicality, before you can possibly turn to aesthetics.

taking a systematic approach

First of all, you have to understand what kind of water supply system your household uses. Do you have hot- and cold-water storage tanks? Are they in the attic or in the basement? Is your water pumped, or does it rely on gravity? Different types of shower are compatible with different plumbing systems, so answering these questions will help you narrow down (or expand) your choice of products. Seek professional advice if you're at all unsure.

under pressure

If you spend a lot of money on an extra-special shower or spa, you don't want to discover that your water supply isn't up to the job. Make sure you find out your water pressure before you choose a shower (your plumber should be able to help), and then check the manufacturer's guidelines about water pressure requirements for any particular shower. Your water pressure will be linked to the type of water supply system you have, and can be boosted by a pump. In general, you'll need at least 0.1 bar of pressure for an adequate shower and 0.6 bar for a strong flow.

less is more

The days of the macho American shower—the kind that doesn't so much wash you as thrash you—are numbered. In recent years U.S. water conservation laws have required that newly installed showerheads be of the low-flow type, capable of delivering a maximum of 21/2 gallons per minute: perfectly adequate but relatively gentle. (Ironically, the notoriously feeble showers once common in Europe are rapidly being replaced by formidable "power showers.") So showers have evolved to offer more in the way of a quality experience. They're safer (see below and 39), more versatile (see 42,) and often more luxurious (see 20, 21).

out of sight

A valve controls the flow of water. This is the part you open and close by turning the handle, dial, or faucet. Choose from an exposed valve, which protrudes from the wall, or a concealed model—buried in the wall and covered with an attractive plate, which sits flush with the surface. Concealed valves are neater looking, and the pipework that runs from the valve to the fixed showerhead is also hidden—ideal for minimalist and contemporary bathrooms.

testing the temperature

Valves are either manual (the action of turning a handle operates the valve) or thermostatic (a thermostat detects changes in temperature and opens and closes the valve automatically to compensate for fluctuations). Thermostatic, or antiscald, valves are more expensive, but they are an excellent safety measure, preventing the cold water from suddenly diverting to another source (for example, when a faucet is turned on) and possibly scalding the person in the shower.

shower stystems

38

Not all showers work in the same way. American showers use a mixer system; that is, a mixer valve blends water from the hot and cold supplies to the desired temperature.

In other parts of the world different systems can be found. The "power shower," now popular in Britain, for example, is similar to a mixer-type system but uses a booster pump to increase the water pressure, providing a high flow. In some models this pump forms part of an all-in-one unit with the shower itself; in others, it is housed in a separate pack, which can be concealed in a closet or next to the water heater.

An electric shower uses only water from the cold supply. This is plumbed over an electrically heated element in a power pack, fixed to the bathroom wall. Although not yet available in the United Sates, this type of shower would be useful wherever only cold water is available, as in some vacation cabins, for example.

shower safety

39

Make sure that your shower is a safe one. The antiscald valve (see 37) is an important safety feature, well worth installing. A much simpler device, but a great boon, especially for anyone with restricted mobility, is the grab bar.

A built-in bench or seat is provided in many modern showers and spas.

modules40

If you want to install a shower in a guest room or another bedroom, the simplest and potentially the least expensive way of doing this is with a shower module. These are all-in-one molded shells, made usually of acrylic or fiberglass, which fit into the designated space and are plumbed into the water supply. (They can, of course, be used in a bathroom, too.) You choose the faucets, showerhead(s), drain, and any other fittings the module is designed to take, making it as traditional or ultramodern in style as you like.

Modules come in various colors, and they vary considerably in size and shape. Some are designed to fit into corners; others fit against a wall or in an alcove. Some also include tubs, and some are designed especially for the disabled. If getting the module into the room would be difficult, you can buy one that comes in several pieces and is assembled on site.

If you're installing a module in a bedroom, you'll need to give some thought to making it "work," both aesthetically and practically. Make sure that the room is well ventilated so that moisture will not be a problem. (A dehumidifier may be advisable.) If the room is carpeted, you may wish to provide a separate area of hard flooring around the shower, which will be easier to clean and dry. If you are opting for a translucent or transparent shower door, you might wish to add a screen in front of the shower for extra privacy and to give this area a sense of separateness. Cover the screen with wallpaper, if this is used on the walls, or with fabric used elsewhere in the room, to integrate the shower area with the room's decor. Or use this fabric as the outer layer of a double shower curtain.

Although this can be used simply for relaxation or therapeutic purposes, it also has a safety function, making a shower a safer option for the elderly or infirm.

And anyone, of any age, can slip on a bar of soap. For peace of mind, use soap on a rope or a liquid soap dipenser.

shower panels

One of the latest trends in bathrooms is the shower panel. It's a wall-mounted console with an integrated array of showerheads and body jets. The complex plumbing for all these outlets is hidden behind the fascia of the console, and all that is required is a simple connection to the hot- and cold-water feeds. It's as easy to disconnect as to connect and this is a very flexible, mobile fixture.

advantages

- Easy "plumb-and-play" installation
- Can go with you when you move
- Superb hydro-massage experience
- Ideal for wet rooms (see 21) but will also fit into larger shower enclosures

disadvantages

- High-pressure water or pump system is required
- High water consumption
- Too bulky for small shower enclosures

Styling of shower panels ranges from boxy models in clinical white acrylic to curvaceous shapes and forms in metallic finishes, colored glass, and even organic wood. Corner models are available, as well as flat-backed panels for wall mounting.

You can customize your shower panel with a choice of a fixed overhead showerhead, a handheld hose, and multiple body jets. Look, too, for useful accessories like lighting, storage shelves on the front, hidden racks or niches behind, and even an integrated radio.

As well as wall-mounted shower panels, you can find floor-standing shower columns, which offer a similar hydro-massage experience. Some columns need wall support behind them, but a few are totally freestanding, and are especially suited to open-plan wet rooms (see 21), for example.

42

showerheads

Although new showerheads deliver less volume than the old ones, they offer a great range of effects. And today it's common to have more than one showerhead, allowing different kinds of shower experiences, from fast and functional to slow and luxurious.

Descending directly from the ceiling, installed on a wall-mounted arm, or wall-mounted at an angle, a fixed showerhead keeps your hands free during showering. However, it's not very flexible in terms of spray direction, and you're likely to get your hair wet even if you don't want to.

A handheld shower is excellent for close-up rinsing and increased flexibility. It's even better if it comes with the option of a glide rail kit, so you can position the showerhead at the angle and height you want, and have both hands free.

Available in polished or matte chrome or nickel finishes, contemporary showerheads tend to be minimalist in style. Choose between pared-down, stick-shaped models (an ideal microphone for singing in the shower!) or overhead showerheads with a 10-inch diameter for a rainfall effect.

Traditional-style showerheads are usually plated in polished brass, gold, or pewter finishes for classical elegance. Styles include the old-fashioned watering-can head and deep-lipped curvaceous showerheads.

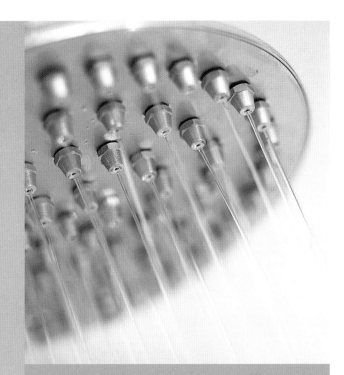

four innovations

Look for these features to increase the functionality of your showerhead.

1 • Adjustable spray patterns: Alternate between powerful pulses, soft rain, or misting sprays
2 • Massagers: Hand-held showerheads with built-in rollers that you rub against your skin
3 • Self-clean heads: Pins push through the holes to clear out mineral deposits
4 • Easy-clean heads: Soft-plastic nozzles quickly rub clean of mineral deposits

43 shower enclosures

While the basic components remain the same—frame, glass panels, door, and base—the new generation of shower enclosures is a far cry from the white plastic box of early days. Design innovation and superior styling create the ultimate showering experience.

glass act

For safety, glass in shower enclosures should always be toughened, and generally at least $1/16$-inch thick. Traditional styles offer patterned or etched glass for privacy, while their contemporary peers promote either crystal-clear panels, tints of gray, green, or blue, or panes sandblasted or acid-etched for opacity. Because soap sediment can cause streaking, look for brands that offer a dirt- and water-repelling coating, to help keep the enclosure looking pristine.

profile piece

The frame, or profile, of the shower is usually offered in basic white or a variety of metallic finishes, including polished and matte chrome or gold. The latest look is a natural, wood-effect finish. The most contemporary versions are stripped of a frame altogether, but this means they lack the flexibility of a framed enclosure which has adjustment potential built into the profiles and hinges to make sure that they can create a watertight fit—even when attached to an out-of-true wall.

five entry types

1 • Sliding door: Is ideal for small bathrooms.

2 • Bi-fold door: Is excellent where space is tight.

3 • Pivot door: Allows a wide entry but swings into the room.

4 • Corner entry: Creates a bigger opening than otherwise possible.

5 • Walk-in entry: No door at all (the screen curves to shield the water).

44

shower floors

Designed to catch water and channel it to the waste pipe, shower floors come in a variety of shapes and sizes. The typical materials are acrylic or fireclay ceramic, but you can also find wood, glass, stone, and resin composites, which open up the color possibilities beyond standard white.

five shower floor shapes

1 • Square (or rectangle): Can look boxy, but good for corners or along one wall.

2 • Quadrant (or off set quadrant): This quarter circle (or elongated quarter circle) fits neatly into a corner and saves space.

3 • Pentangle or neo-angle: A five-sided base, suits corners in small bathrooms.

4 • Circle: Usually a freestanding design; looks exciting, but does need space.

5 • Contoured: A contoured edge adds interest to a square or rectangular design (often seen in walk-in enclosures).

45

steam cabinets

Unlike a shower enclosure, which is open at the top, a steam cabin is a completely sealed unit with floor, glass panels, door, and roof. This creates a watertight cocoon where you can indulge in hydrotherapy at home (see 20).

A basic shower enclosure will include a fixed overhead shower and/or a handheld shower on a glide rail. Hydro-massage versions add multiple targeted body jets, while spa-style steam cabinets offer a Turkish bath experience, which will cleanse your pores, detoxify your body, and clear your airways. Other indulgences include aromatherapy diffusers, colored lights (chromotherapy), music systems, infra-red heat—and, of course, a comfortable seat. The best and biggest models are double cabinets for shared pleasure.

46 bathroom sink basics

The sink is a fundamental bathroom fixture, a water receptacle for easy cleansing of hands and face. But from its basic origins—a simple bowl to hold water—it has evolved into a sophisticated and design-conscious bathroom centerpiece.

raison d'être

The first question you should ask yourself is what purpose your sink will serve. Is it for hand-washing only? Or also where you'll wash your face, and even your hair, or brush your teeth? How you use the sink will help you decide what size and shape you need.

dare to be different

The days of matching bathroom fixtures are gone. Make the sink a focal point, featuring unusual materials such as glass, stainless steel, or wood, rather than white ceramic (see 47).

support structure

There are three principal ways to support a sink: on a pedestal, set into or on top of a piece of furniture, or fixed to a wall. Each of these alternative approaches has advantages and drawbacks, so consider the practical implications when making your decision (see 48–50).

follow the lines

Sinks with strong rectilinear shapes look stunning, but curved bowls may be more practical. Remember that sharp internal angles will make cleaning your sink more difficult (see 51).

lime aid

If your bathroom suffers from lime deposits, unless you're prepared to clean the sink every day to maintain its shiny finish, opt for a slick, easy-clean surface, and a shape that prevents water from pooling at the bottom or on ledges around the sides.

shallow waters

If you live in an area where there is high water pressure, a shallow sink might prove impractical, forcing the water to splash and swirl out. In addition, the positioning of the faucet can exacerbate the amount of splashing. Consider a deeper sink with a gentler slope, and perhaps a faucet with a flow restrictor to mitigate the problem.

easy reach

Not all sink designs incorporate wide ledges where you can rest a bar of soap or anything else you like at hand. Wall-mounted soap dishes or liquid soap dispensers, special toothbrush holders, and glass shelving bring essential items within reach and keep sink ledges clear for easy cleaning.

two's company

In a private bath shared by a couple, it's always worth considering installing two sinks, side by side, if there is space available. Just think: no more banging elbows or waiting impatiently to brush your teeth!

go with the overflow

Although most sinks have an overflow (which makes sure that if the faucet is left running with the plug in, there won't be a flood), not all do. Check the model you are buying. An overflow is vital if there are children in the house—or absentminded adults!

waste not

There are several alternatives to the old plastic plug on a chain, one of them being the pop-up drain. A lever on the adjustable faucet operates the metal plug, keeping lines clean and surfaces smooth. Also the spin waste (which sits in the plughole and swivels open or closed when you touch it). Although it looks very minimalist and neat, it has a drawback: you have to plunge your hand into dirty water to operate it.

10 ideas

material world

ceramic

Vitreous china sinks offer an extensive choice of sizes, styles, and shapes.

advantages
• Non-porous and hygienic
• Easy to clean, particularly with special glazes that repel water and dirt
• Wide range of prices

disadvantages
• Will chip or crack if you drop something heavy onto it

stone

Marble and limestone can appear refined or rustic, depending on how the stone is worked.

advantages
• Often made to order, so you can specify the shape, size, and style

disadvantages
• Porous (sinks will need resealing approximately every six months)
• Heavy: Will need strong supports

wood

Wooden sinks are usually made from hardwood or marine ply and come in a variety of designs.

advantages
• Softens hard-edged designs
• Hardwoods such as teak are naturally antibacterial

disadvantages
• Wood needs to be sealed and maintained to keep it watertight
• The wood can split if it dries out too much

glass

Beautiful clear or frosted sinks are created from tempered glass or laminated safety glass.

advantages
• Appears light and airy, so works well in small spaces
• Non-porous and hygienic

disadvantages
• Shows splashmarks, toothpaste, lime deposits, etc

composite

Made from a mix of crushed minerals and resin, composites are molded into seamless basins in all shapes and sizes.

advantages
• Hundreds of color choices
• Can be seamlessly integrated into a composite countertop

disadvantages
• May stain if not cleaned

stainless steel

Reminiscent of prison cells and hospitals, stainless steel sinks are sure to add an industrial note to a bathroom.

advantages
• Extremely hygienic

disadvantages
• Shows water marks

48 counter-mounted

The counter in question might be a piece of built-in furniture, a freestanding bureau, or even a cantilevered shelf.

Some typical placement styles:
• **Lotus-mounted**: The bowl perches on top of the counter
• **Semi-inset**: The bowl is set into the counter, with the front edge protruding
• **Undermounted**: The bowl is set below the surface of the counter
• **Integrated**: The bowl joins seamlessly with the counter—for example, in the case of a glass or composite option

A surrounding counter gives you the benefit of storage around the sink, and the pipework will be hidden if the furniture has doors.

49 on a pedestal

Pedestal sinks typically comprise a ceramic bowl sitting on a matching ceramic pedestal, which runs to the floor. This pedestal has a dual function, as it conceals the pipework beneath the basin, but also supports the weight of the heavy ceramic bowl.

In terms of design, the shape of the pedestal will usually echo the style of the ceramic bowl, taking on either traditional or contemporary detailing. Occasionally, you'll find a combination of materials used to stunning effect, such as a glass or ceramic bowl perched on a stainless steel leg.

Although pedestal basins look neat and clean, you will find that dust and dirt gather at the base, which is tricky to clean behind.

50 wall-mounted

The trend for wall-mounting the sink rather than using a supporting pedestal continues to grow. It's not suitable for all bathrooms, though, as a heavy sink will require a strong wall to bear the weight.

advantages
• Keeps the floor clear for cleaning
• Makes the room feel more spacious
• Can be set at whatever height you want

disadvantages
• Requires structural work to install support frame
• Wall may need to be strengthened

Bear in mind, too, that the pipes and waste trap will be visible. You can either conceal these with a ceramic semi-pedestal or stainless steel shroud, or pay extra for chrome-plated feature plumbing.

51

shapes and sizes

If you're plagued by indecision as you survey the vast choice of sink shapes and sizes, make your selection based on practical design parameters—what fits where? what's easy to clean?—as well as personal preferences.

round and curved

Designs based on the form of a circle are big news at the moment. Whether it's a round glass bowl perched on a vanity unit or a ceramic sink on a full-length pedestal, curves add a soft note to a bathroom. They tend to be easy to clean, as there are no internal corners where dirt can collect.

strictly straight

Seemingly inspired by old-fashioned sinks, many bathroom sinks display rectilinear geometry. In ceramic or stone, these trough-like rectangles and squares share the same heavy proportions and robust styling as their kitchen cousins, and are often found perched on wooden

seeing double 52

It's not unusual for a couple to use an en-suite bathroom together, and in a family bathroom, you'll often see several children crowding in at one time. Elbows tend to get knocked and tempers are likely to get particularly frayed around the sink.

Imagine the luxury of being able to brush your teeth in a leisurely manner, not worrying about hands darting in to turn your cold water hot—or someone aiming poorly when they spit out their toothpaste! The ideal solution is to have twin sinks.

Obviously, your plans may be halted by space limitations. In a small bathroom, you're struggling to fit in a sink, bathtub, and toilet, let alone an additional item. In which case, try at least to keep your single basin relatively free of obstacles around it, so that two people can stand at either side.

In a medium-size bathroom, compromise comes in the form of a wide sink, where two people can comfortably stand next to each other. You can even find one-piece basins that are divided internally to form two separate sinks.

And if you're fortunate to have a generous amount of space, look at placing twin bowls on a long vanity unit (see 66) or standing matching pedestal basins side by side. Yes, you'll double your costs on the sinks, the wastes, and the faucets, but the benefits you gain in terms of convenience—and time saved during an early morning bathroom rush—make it worth it.

counters or wall-mounted for an architectural look. Internal angles can harbor dirt and make cleaning a little more difficult.

best of both worlds

A mixture of straight lines and curved edges defines most sink designs, particularly the traditional D-shape of the ceramic pedestal basin.

cornerwise

Quadrant-shaped corner sinks are a great solution in a small bathroom. Slotting into a right angle of the room, the corner sink makes use of an otherwise wasted space.

big and little

Sinks vary greatly in size and shape. The typical hand basin measures about 15 x 12 inches, whereas trough-style sinks may measure up to 30 inches wide. Of equal importance is the projection of the sink. A large sink may project 2 feet into the room, a compact version only 15 inches, and a tiny hand-rinse sink perhaps only a foot or less.

fabulous faucets

A small detail like a faucet can make or break a design, so be prepared to spend time—and money—on that perfect accessory. You want beautiful form, a design that won't date too quickly, and a degree of functionality that will make your life as easy as possible.

old and new

If your bathroom scheme is classical, it makes sense to choose a period-style fitting, such as Art Deco or Victorian. But it can also be fun to play with design a little. For example, you could choose a faucet that makes reference to old designs (e.g., a bridge faucet—see 54) but offers a contemporary silver-finish (such as matte chrome—see 55). And if you do opt for something ultramodern for your contemporary bathroom, don't sacrifice functionality. Some designs pare the form down so much that the controllability is sacrificed (can you grip that tiny lever?).

under pressure

Before you buy a faucet, find out your water pressure (see 8). Many designs are suited to high-pressure systems only. Others are specific to low pressure, so be sure you know what you're buying—mistakes can be costly. Also ask your plumber if your hot and cold water are balanced. Certain systems function properly only if there's equal pressure in both feeds.

eco-aware

In this environmentally conscious age, some manufacturers are helping us save water. If you have a high-pressure system, look for a faucet with an aerator. This metal mesh restricts the flow of water and oxygenates it to produce a bubbly flow that feels "bigger" than it actually is.

take cover

If you are buying a high-quality faucet—and paying a lot of money for it—you expect it to last. Check that the faucet is covered by a product warranty (generally 5–10 years) to give you peace of mind.

faucet facts

• Ceramic disks: Increasingly, ceramic disk valves are replacing the traditional screw-down valve and rubber washer. (A valve is the part of the faucet that opens and closes to allow water through.) A ceramic disk allows a full flow of water with minimum movement (usually only a quarter-turn from off to fully on) and is much more durable than rubber washers, which tend to wear away and cause the faucet to leak.

However, be slightly cautious if you are in a hard-water area. A ceramic disk can be damaged by excessive particles of limescale or other sediments—and unlike a rubber washer, it's not cheap to replace.

• Thermostatic, or antiscald, valves: A thermostatic valve reacts to changes in the water temperature, so if the cold flow is suddenly diverted (to the washing machine, for example), it immediately reduces the hot water flow to prevent scalding. It can be set to maintain a temperature you find comfortable. You are more likely to find these on a bathtub faucet than a sink faucet (see 54), as they tend to be linked to bath/shower systems.

• Infrared sensors: If you can't decide between a lever or a traditional cross head to turn on your faucet, why not go for the ultimate in technology—an infrared, hands-free faucet? Moving out of the hospitality sector and into the private bathroom, these turn on and off with a wave of the hand and are extremely hygienic!

54 faucet styles

Old-fashioned sinks used to have separate hot and cold faucets, instead of the modern single faucet with adjustable water temperature. While some older homes retain these as a design feature, the convenience of adjustable faucets is clear. In plumbing terms there are several kinds.

faucet construction

• One-hole or monobloc: The spout and controls (which may be handles, heads, or levers) form part of a single unit
• Two-hole: The spout is separate from the single control, which operates both temperature and flow rate
• Three-hole: The spout and the hot and cold controls are all separate units

55 faucet finishes

Faucets and shower fittings have traditionally been made of brass, which is then plated with a hardwearing and attractive metal finish, silver or gold in color.

Silver-colored faucets are commonly plated in chrome or nickel, though platinum, aluminum, steel, and even genuine silver-plating can be found. The latest trend in silver metals sees polished surfaces being superseded by matte or satin finishes. These hide splash marks better and are easier to clean.

Gold-colored faucets are generally perceived as being a traditional choice, and sometimes even a little glitzy. The finish itself might be real gold (true indulgence!) or, more commonly, polished brass or a brass alloy. These yellow metals are all quite soft, so will scratch and

• Bridge: The hot and cold pipes join in a bridge shape, with a central spout for the blended water

It's important to test a faucet before you buy. How does it feel? Can it be gripped with a soapy hand? A simple cross-head design is probably the most effective in this regard, but for ease of use—particularly if you suffer from arthritis, for example—try out a lever style. You don't need nimble fingers or particular strength to push it on and off, though it can be tricky to adjust the flow rate or temperature precisely.

A simple head that crowns the faucet can form a joystick-style control. The streamlined look is excellent on modern and minimal styles, and it means there are no fussy bits to clean. However, as with lever taps, a degree of precision is needed to find the right temperature and water flow—and even to return the head to the off-position.

eventually may show signs of wear. But gold-hued faucets have a visual warmth, which is lacking in silver-colored faucets.

top brass

• Solid brass is reassuringly heavy. If you pick up a faucet that feels light in your hand, put it back down and walk away. Don't let a cheap and flimsy plastic faucet spoil your bathroom.
• For a super-hard exterior, look for PVD (physical vapor deposition), a process that bonds a finish to the faucet and protects the metal-plating, and is claimed to be eight times harder than chrome and twice as hard as steel.
• Some faucets incorporate more than one metal or texture in the finish—for example, gold accents on chrome or a mixture of polished and matte metals of the same color.

56

faucets in position

The design of your bathtub or sink may influence where you put your faucet. Some come pre-drilled with holes, and although you can cap these off, it can look slightly "amateur" and can spoil the smooth lines of the sink or tub.

Old bathtubs might have only two holes provided, but you don't have to settle for old-fashioned faucets that supply hot and cold water separately (see 54). You could, for example, choose a bridge faucet (see 54) or have an extra hole drilled for a central spout.

If you're buying a brand-new bathtub or sink, you may be given the option of choosing how many holes—if any—you want, and where you want them. For the streamlined look that a wall-mounted sink offers, opt for no holes. But if you want to top-mount your faucet, ask yourself whether you want them to perch on the rim of the tub or sink, or to sit alongside on, for example, a tiled counter. And do you want the faucet positioned centrally or at the foot end of the bath, or offset at one side of the sink?

wall-mounted

Wall-mounted faucets protrude from the wall, with the horizontal spout projecting over the bathtub or sink.

advantages
• Easier to clean the sink or bath
• No water (or mineral deposits) pooling at base
• Clean-lined look; pipes are buried in wall

disadvantages
• Early planning required (or you'll have to rip tiles off wall)
• If sink or tub does not butt up against the wall, the water from your hand will drip onto the countertop or bath surround

top-mounted

Top-mounted faucets stand vertically on the rim of the bathtub or sink, or closely alongside on a counter, for example.

advantages

• No disruption of walls to bury pipes, and therefore less expensive and less time-consuming to install
• Easier to access if there are problems
• Easier to change
• Sink faucets can be positioned wherever suits you best—left, right, or center

disadvantages

• More difficult to clean the bathtub or sink (or countertop)
• Water can collect around the base, causing staining and mold

floor-mounted

Floor-mounted faucets are elevated on risers or standpipes that run to the floor.

advantages

• A great solution for a free-standing bathtub, or even for a sink positioned away from the wall

disadvantages

• You'll drip water on the floor as you reach for the faucet with wet hands
• You'll need to run the plumbing under the floor

Think about the projection of your tub or sink spout. As you lean over a basin to wash your face, you don't want to bang your head on a long spout. Likewise, if you're positioning the tub faucets at the center of the long edge (which makes particular sense if you've opted for a double-ended bathtub [see 27] for shared bathing—no more arguments about who gets the faucet end!), a long faucet could encroach on your showering area, for example. But on the other hand, you don't want the water to dribble down the side of the bathtub or sink. Go for a happy medium.

first impressions

If at all possible, don't make the toilet the first thing you see when you open the bathroom door. Unfortunately, you may be restricted by the size and shape of your bathroom, or by the positioning of the waste pipe. The toilet needs to connect to this pipe, which carries waste and water away. It can be expensive to move the waste pipe and difficult to extend it.

in a tight corner

If space is limited, look for a compact toilet. Better yet, conceal the cistern within the wall, so only the bowl juts into the room. An unusual solution is a corner model with a triangular cistern, which slots neatly into otherwise dead space.

feeling flushed

Think of the water you use every time you flush. Thankfully, you have the option of environmentally conscious, dual-flush mechanisms. These allow for a water-conserving, half-flush option, which uses less than a gallon of water. For a pared-down look and ease of use, choose a discreet push-button system rather than a handle.

deep clean

Cleaning the toilet is no one's idea of fun—but at least some models make life a little easier. Some manufacturers offer special pore-free ceramics and water-repellent glazes, which help keep the inner bowl more free of limescale and germs. Also, look for toilet seats that are designed to clip on and off for easy-access cleaning.

ups and downs

It's the age-old argument between men and women. And it's been solved by technology. There are now toilets available with hydraulically operated, self-closing seats, which slowly lower themselves after use. The expense might be worth it, if it saves disagreements!

bathroom basics

It may not be glamorous, but the toilet fulfills the most basic of purposes in the bathroom. Hygiene, accessibility, comfort, and practicality are all important considerations.

the toilet

The current trend is for ultra-clean, clinically white toilets. Lines are sleek and pared-down, a look that not only complements the modern bathroom but also minimizes nooks and crannies where germs can breed. Where and how you position the toilet will also have a great bearing on the look of your bathroom.

one-piece

The cistern and bowl are joined in one complete unit, with the cistern visible above and behind the bowl. This requires no structural work to install, but looks bulky, and it can be tricky to clean around the pedestal.

back-to-wall

A separate cistern is concealed in a wall or within built-in furniture, and the bowl butts up against this wall or furniture. Structural alterations can be expensive, and you must ensure that the cistern can still be accessed (see 62). The look is streamlined and appears to enlarge small bathrooms.

wall hung

The toilet, without pedestal, is cantilevered from the wall (see 13). You will require a support bracket, and in some cases, the wall will need to be strengthened to bear the weight. Back-to-wall, wall-hung models offer the ultimate minimalist look, visually create more space, and make it extremely easy to clean the floor underneath. It also means you can choose the height of the seat, which is good if you're extra tall (or short).

to bidet or not to bidet?

Whether you choose to have a bidet in your bathroom will, in part, depend on your upbringing and where you live. The bidet, viewed with derision and suspicion by some, is seen as an everyday hygienic necessity by others.

The bidet sits alongside the toilet, and most often it will be a partner piece, with the same design detailing. You can even get toilet and bidet models with matching seats for a fully coordinating look.

And like the toilet, the bidet can be wall mounted, which helps the room to open up visually. In addition, this means that the floor is more accessible and easier to keep pristine.

separate lives 60

Although most American homes feature main bathrooms with integrated toilet, bathtub, sink, and shower, there is a strong argument for having a toilet in a separate room, European-style. Think about how you use your home, how many people live there, how often people visit—and then imagine the increased flexibility if your bathroom and toilet are two separate entities.

• Your relaxing bath will no longer be interrupted by anyone knocking urgently at the door.
• The early-morning line outside the bathroom door will be reduced—one child can be brushing his or her teeth at the sink while the other is using the toilet next door.
• If you have guests staying, they'll feel less anxious that they may be inconveniencing you while they're in the bathroom.

Creating a separate toilet area can be as simple as erecting a partition wall within the bathroom, and installing another door accessed from the hallway.

However, not all bathroom layouts will allow this simple but effective solution. In which case, could the space necessary for the toilet be borrowed from an adjacent room? Or could a nearby closet be converted into a toilet area? Obviously, these structural alterations will be costly, messy, and time-consuming, and you must take into account the potential problems associated with moving or extending a waste pipe. You'll also need to provide a small sink for hand washing; so you're actually creating an adjacent powder room. If you don't already have a powder room in your house, it's well worth adding one—even if you choose to include a toilet in your main bathroom. For one thing, a spare toilet is a godsend when you next do a complete bathroom renovation and all your fixtures are ripped out!

privacy, please

61

In a family home, or with a couple sharing, privacy in the bathroom can become a precious and much-missed commodity. The door is often left unlocked, or even open, and it's common for the room to be used by more than one person at a time. But sometimes it's nice to have a little privacy.

If it's not possible to create a separate toilet area, screening off the toilet within the bathroom goes at least some way to establishing a private zone. This can be done in such a way that the partition becomes a positive design feature.

a glass screen

A sheet of frosted glass, supported by brackets or cemented in place, offers a good level of opacity to discreetly conceal the toilet, but it has the benefit of being translucent, so light won't be obstructed.

a wall of glass blocks

Like a glass screen, this offers privacy without blocking the light. It is also relatively easy to install and can be built by a proficient amateur.

a partition wall

A half-wall or ceiling-high partition effectively screens the toilet area from the rest of the bathroom. Alcoves can be built into the wall to offer display storage, accessible from either side of the partition. These alcoves also make the wall seem less imposing.

hideaways

Cabinets are the staple of bathroom storage and come in all sizes, shapes, materials, and colors. You can choose built-in furniture, freestanding units, or wall-mounted cabinets, with a variety of compartments and drawers inside. But there are many more options that help you tidy away the bathroom clutter.

freewheeling

A wheeled unit gives you maximum flexibility within your bathroom design. Tuck it neatly away beneath the sink or alongside the bathtub whenever it's not in use, and pull it out into the open when you need to access the contents.

good medicine

The medicine cabinet keeps pills, tablets, bottles of medicine, and first-aid equipment together in one safe place, out of children's hands. You can find versions that are clearly medicine-specific (with a red cross on the front, for example) or simply use a small general-purpose wall cabinet with a door—and preferably a lock.

between the walls

If you have a small bathroom, every inch of space is important. Consider setting alcoves into the walls, to a depth of about 4 inches, to create a shallow storage recess.

blissful bathing

If you set the bathtub into a furniture surround, you'll create a perimeter shelf, where your soaps and body scrubs can sit within immediate reach. No more having to clamber, dripping wet, out of a hot bath to get them from a cabinet.

rack it up

Within reach of the shower or bathtub, you're bound to need a selection of shampoos and shower gels and a variety of sponges and loofahs. Wall-mount chrome- or brass-plated baskets, or install a rack with compartments designed to hold all those necessities at hand.

hideaways

As an alternative to concealing a toilet cistern in a false wall, you can hide it away inside specially designed furniture. Slim units run from the floor to just above cistern height, creating a streamlined look with a push-button flush. A removable panel on the front or top allows access to the cistern for maintenance.

bin it

Tired of picking clothes off the bathroom floor? A laundry bin certainly makes life easier. The traditional wicker basket is now rivaled by smart wooden and metal freestanding containers, some of which double as seats. An alternative is to conceal the laundry bin, often a strong linen bag or a wire mesh container, within a closet.

basket cases

Add an organic note to a bathroom with baskets woven from willow or cane. Stack them on the floor with piles of towels inside, place them on shelves to discreetly hold spare toilet paper, or put them in closets to compartmentalize the interior.

reading material

Instead of letting magazines and newspapers clutter up the floor, opt for a wall-mounted magazine holder, or a stylish multipurpose rack that also includes a toilet paper holder and a toilet brush.

safe and secure

As well as storing cleansing lotions and potions for your body, you'll often want to keep bathroom cleaning agents, detergents, and bleach close at hand. For these, you'll need concealed storage (they're not the most attractive bottles) and preferably a lockable cabinet if you have young children in the house.

63 furniture features

Bathroom furniture used to be unimaginative and unvaried: an imposing bank of white fixtures, with fussy detailing and yet a blandly uniform appearance. The reality now, amid ranges of built-in, freestanding, and modular furniture, is an exciting choice of colors and materials, with slick exterior finishes and intelligent internal storage solutions.

Materials vary, but wood retains its popularity, either painted or with its grain exposed. Lacquered finishes are available in many colors. For a striking effect, there is acid-etched glass or matte aluminum paneling. Work surfaces are high-performance to protect against moisture and knocks and scratches. Solid surface composites, high-pressure laminates with waterproof backing, and toughened glass are some of the principal options.

Most ranges present the opportunity of external accessories like backsplashes, lighting, and mirrors. Obviously, these extras add to the price, but they do help provide complete solutions for your bathroom needs.

The variety of internal storage solutions for bathroom furniture now rivals that of the kitchen. When you open the doors you'll find corner carousels, pull-out racks, integrated laundry bins, wastebaskets, and compartmentalized drawers, all

designed to conceal your bathroom clutter behind a calm exterior.

access all areas

Check that the bathroom furniture you buy incorporates access panels so that your plumbing can be checked and maintained with the minimum of fuss. You should be able to quickly unscrew or unclip the panel to reach the pipes beneath the bathtub or sink, or the cistern of your back-to-wall toilet.

built-in furniture

The days of solid banks of cabinets overpowering a bathroom design are gone. Now, built-in furniture is trying not to look so . . . built-in. Yes, you can still opt for a run of base cabinets stretching from wall to wall, but it's much more visually stimulating to mix and match using a selection of versatile pieces.

base units

These floor-standing cabinets are the staple elements of any range of built-in furniture. For a less heavy look, opt for plinth-free designs with stylish chrome legs, or a recessed plinth that gives the impression of "floating." You can even wall-mount units to free up the floor, making the room feel more spacious (see 13) and making cleaning easier. Select a variety of depths, depending on how much space you have and whether you want to install a sink. You can also vary the "skyline" with a range of heights.

wall units

Head-height storage is easy to access (and can keep things out of children's hands). To make wall units seem less uniform and imposing, select a variety of heights, widths, and depths. Use frosted-glass doors for a lighter look, and consider how they will open—sliding doors or upward bi-folding doors will be more space-saving.

small concerns

If you have a small bathroom, your first thought may be that squeezing in furniture will make the space even more cramped. However, built-in furniture can have the opposite effect. Use a bank of units with a depth of about 8 inches to conceal the toilet cistern, to hide away pipes, and to form a support for a semi-inset sink. Streamlining one wall of the room can make the space appear deceptively large.

freestanding furniture

65

The popularity of freestanding bathroom furniture lies in its flexibility. Different elements can be moved around the room if your needs change—or if you simply want to try a different layout. You can bring in new items as and when you can afford them, or if you decide later that you need more storage. And when you move, you can take this furniture with you.

Another reason to choose freestanding pieces is that a few select elements can look less imposing than a traditional, wall-to-wall bank of built-in cabinets (though with the varied looks of the latest collections of built-in bathroom furniture, the distinction between freestanding and built-in has become extremely blurred).

Prime pieces of freestanding furniture for your bathroom might include
• low sets of pull-out drawers—ideal for towels, and useful to sit on too
• wheeled units that can be pulled out from under sinks or pushed next to the bathtub whenever you need a "bathside" table
• armoires with lots of shelving inside for bottles and boxes
• sink stations—a bureau or table that supports a sink and provides storage beneath (see 66)
• laundry bins, so dirty clothes and wet towels aren't left lying on the floor
• storage chests—ideal for towels, and they make great seats, too

It's common for ranges of bathroom furniture to offer both freestanding and built-in items, allowing you to create a modular look in your bathroom. Imagine a bank of wall-fixed built-in base units with a complementary laundry bin or matching wheeled unit that can be moved wherever you wish.

66 vanity units

As its name suggests, the vanity unit is the area of the bathroom dedicated to primping and preening. For women, it has replaced the bedroom dressing table. And for men? Well, give them a mirror and they can beautify with the best of them!

The basic elements of a vanity unit are a mirror, good lighting, a sink, and handy storage. By bringing together these four elements, you can create your own personal beauty and grooming zone.

sink stations

A sink station is a dual-function piece of furniture that combines a bathroom sink with storage solutions. In its basic form it's a table with a sink set on or in it. The tabletop around the sink serves as an easily accessed area for soap, toothbrushes, make-up, etc., and shelving beneath keeps larger items at hand. A towel holder at the front or side is a useful additional feature.

67 on the wall, in the wall

It's common to see cabinets and shelves attached to a wall, but you can also make use of the space within the wall itself to create shelving recesses or feature alcoves.

why use walls?
- Clears the floor area for a sense of space
- Storage can be fixed at eye-level height
- Items can be placed out of reach of children

Shelves are one of the simplest forms of storage. Choose narrow glass shelves on chrome brackets, hefty wooden slabs on wrought-iron supports, or gloss-painted thick particleboard, cantilevered from the wall. It's best to combine shelving with cabinets, so you can hide away general bathroom paraphernalia; otherwise be prepared to keep everything neat. Folded towels and attractive bottles can look stylish.

mirrored cabinets

A mirrored wall unit above the sink is invaluable for applying make-up, shaving, or putting in contact lenses. Look for one with integrated lighting and outlets (for an electric razor or an electric toothbrush), but remember that it will need to be wired in.

waterproofing your walls 68

It makes sense to choose a finish for your bathroom walls that will withstand steam and humidity, occasional splashes and drips—or even regular torrents of water. Before you make your decision, consider the points listed below.

how wet will it get?

The first question to ask yourself is how much water will come into contact with your walls. Areas near the sink and bathtub are bound to suffer occasional splashes, for example, even if adults are using them. If children are involved, the splashes will be more frequent—and bigger! And the walls of a shower enclosure must be fully waterproofed, of course. Also, take account of the effects of steam. If you (and other members of your family) have long, hot showers every day, the bathroom will be frequently exposed to humidity. Clouds of steam will condense into tiny water droplets on cold surfaces such as walls.

mix and match

Experiment with mixing different wall coverings according to where the water will splash. One popular approach is the half-tiled wall, where an area up to about head height is tiled, and the rest of the wall painted. Alternatively, you could create a neat backsplash behind the sink or on the wall next to the bathtub—use tiles, wood, glass, stone, or laminate—and apply a contrasting wall covering elsewhere. It's a cost-effective way of waterproofing vulnerable zones, and you can opt for more expensive materials for your backsplash since you aren't covering such a large area.

papering over

Generally, wallpaper is not recommended for bathrooms (with the exception of a few specialized moisture-resistant papers). If you have excellent ventilation and low humidity—and if you promise not to splash!—then yes, you can paper the walls. Otherwise, don't be surprised if the paper peels, stains, or mildews within a matter of months.

going solo

Most people are capable of picking up a paintbrush, some can even master tiling, but stone cladding or plaster finishes really are best left to the experts. And professional labor costs money (see 4 and 5). If you're not prepared to learn how to tile a bathroom, or don't have time, you could be looking at two or three days' labor on top of the initial cost of the tiles. Plaster finishes may be quicker to apply, but finishing them (waxing and polishing) also adds on hours of labor. Always factor in the costs of installation when making your decision.

last, but not least

It can be tempting to forge ahead with preparing and decorating the walls to give your room a finished look. But remember that you may have to gouge out sections of wall to bury pipes or wiring. In your schedule of completion, wall finishes are a cosmetic consideration and should be one of the last items you tackle (see 25 and 26).

69
ceramic tiles

Ceramic tiles are made from a mixture of clays and other minerals, which are shaped and fired to create a stable material. Over centuries, the ancient craft of tile making has evolved to encompass new manufacturing processes and technological developments, and the diversity of ceramic tiles is now astonishing. Designs embrace a myriad colors, sizes, patterns, and shapes.

Ceramic tiles fall into two broad categories: glazed and unglazed. Wall tiles are generally glazed, which means they are coated with a non-porous, protective vitreous coating.

five benefits of glazed tiles

1 • unlimited color variations
2 • stain resistance
3 • superior waterproofing
4 • extremely hygienic
5 • easy to clean

wall or floor?

Manufacturers usually specify whether tiles are suitable for walls or for floors. Floor tiles are often too thick and heavy to apply to walls, and wall tiles are too delicate to withstand foot traffic—so make sure you're buying tiles suited to the purpose.

Once grouted in place, tiles cannot be removed without breaking. So be cautious if you're following a specific color trend that may date quickly. Aqueous blues and greens seem to be standing the test of time, however, and white is a classic choice.

Don't just think about color, but consider size, shape, and texture, too. All have a bearing on the look of a room. Larger squares can open a room up more, while rectangles running vertically will make a room appear taller. Texture is also very important. It can add visual interest to a solid color such as white, and provide tactile interest when you touch the tiles. However, it's best to opt for a subtle texture that won't harbor dirt or germs.

mosaic tiles

Roman villas and Byzantine palaces were decorated with mosaic pictures composed of thousands of tiny tiles. Interest in mosaics has been renewed recently, though the elaborate designs of past eras are rarely re-created. It's more usual to cover the walls in mosaic tiles (or tesserae, as they're known) of a single color or varying shades of one color, such as a palette of blues. To make application easier, mosaic tiles usually come in web-backed sheets, containing perhaps 100 tiles or more, so they don't have to be applied individually.

mosaic magic

• Look for mosaic tiles in stone, metal, and glass, as well as ceramic.

• If you find the look of a whole bathroom or wall covered in mosaic tiles overpowering, why not use just a narrow strip of mosaics to define an area?

• Try popping a tile out, at random, from each sheet of mosaic, and replacing it with a single tile of a contrasting color.

glass and metal tiles

71

Glass and metal tiles have found their place in bathrooms as a complement to the materials that are being incorporated into bathroom design. Acid-etched glass screens, frosted sinks, sandblasted shelves, and other accessories can be accented by the use of glass tiles in matching subtle hues. Or you can pick out the gleam of polished chrome shower fittings or the duller sheen of satin-finished faucets using tiles with bright silver surfaces.

Some glass tiles are pigmented throughout, while others simply have a colored backing. You'll find different degrees of tone and translucency; bear in mind that when applied to a wall, the tiles will lose some of their luster and may appear to be darker than you first imagined.

Metal tiles are usually ceramic tiles with a metallic glaze, though you may come across some solid metal plates that function as tiles. Silver hues include platinum, stainless steel, nickel, pewter, and chrome, but for more warmth choose gold, copper, or brass.

It's worth noting that some metals, such as copper and brass, will tarnish unless they are protected by a lacquer coating, and that all metals will scratch if rubbed with an abrasive cleaner and will be damaged by acids, such as some cleansing agents.

wooden paneling

The term "wooden paneling" may bring to mind dark and dusty old libraries, but in the bathroom environment, it is typically blond wood tongue-and-groove that is used (so called because of the way the boards slot together—a protruding tongue on one fits into a precut groove on the next). Tongue-and-groove has an organic and simple feel and is associated with a robust, outdoorsy aesthetic. Leaving knotted pine, for example, in its naked state (apart from a clear varnish sealant) creates a very raw and natural-looking bathroom.

Because wood has to be protected from moisture, paint can be used instead of varnish to seal it. Choose a gloss or satin version that is specific to wood—and will resist damp conditions. Color choices are extensive, though white is always popular, and aqueous blues and greens often feature, especially in marine-themed bathrooms.

Tongue-and-groove is commonly applied to mid- or even three-quarter-height on the walls, but it can be overpowering if used too extensively. Although it's a cost-effective way of covering expanses of wall, be restrained and reserve it for small sections, such as behind the bathtub, and even for the box surround.

new wood

Modernists have abandoned gently old-fashioned tongue-and-groove in favor of veneers of rich cherrywood, grained oak, and patterned walnut, which are securely fixed to walls and sealed with waterproof lacquer. Equally striking are panels of tropical hardwoods, like iroko and teak. But these water-resistant woods don't come cheap and need occasional re-sealing if they are used close to water. If at all possible, be environmentally responsible and make sure your wood (especially the more exotic species) has been sourced from sustainable forests.

stone surfaces

Stone is so versatile that it is difficult to define it categorically. It can be rustic or refined, traditional or modern, easy-wear or high-maintenance. The only qualities that can be commonly ascribed to all types of stone are durability and unchangeability.

Unlike ceramic tiles, those made of stone are not designed by man. The characteristics of each type of stone are "designed" by nature, formed millennia upon millennia ago. All we can affect is the shape and size of tile that is cut from the huge sheets and boulders of rock quarried from the earth. After processing, the resultant cladding material ranges from weighty slabs to tiny mosaic tesserae (see 70).

Bathroom walls tend to feature four main families of stone: granite, marble, limestone, and slate. Each has a particular aesthetic, so the choice will be based as much on personal likes and dislikes as on any practical reasoning.

granite

• Extremely hardwearing and practical
• Impervious to water
• Mottled or flecked in appearance
• Wide spectrum of colors, particularly darker shades, including black, red, brown, and green

marble

• Associated with classical and opulent ambiance
• Porous, needs to be sealed
• Usually veined in appearance
• Pure marble is white, but other shades (grays, browns, reds, even black) are also found

limestone

• Offers a calm, soothing, contemporary look
• High porosity, needs to be sealed
• Generally uniform appearance, some slight mottling or fossilization
• Commonly found in golden, buff, and sandy tones, but also white, gray, blue, or even chocolate brown

slate

• Works particularly well with rustic or ethnic style
• Waterproof
• Usually a textured surface, crystalline glints, some striping or mottling
• Generally charcoal gray, with blue, purple and green variations

Make sure you explain to your supplier that the stone you choose

is for use on walls. Stone is extremely heavy, so your wall covering needs to be as thin and light as possible. Regular-sized, wall-specific tiles are easier to use than large slabs, but even so, are best applied by professionals, who can ensure that sufficiently strong cement is used. If you want the sophisticated look that outsized slabs offer, you may need your wall strengthened, and the slabs will have to be fixed to a special support system.

The whole look of your bathroom will be defined not only by the type of stone you choose—and the size and shape of the tile—but also by the finish given to the stone. A highly polished finish suggests opulence and glamour and works well with granite and marble; a honed finish (matte-satin) is more subtle and modern, but offers a similarly wipe-clean surface; textured finishes caused by tumbling, bush-hammering, or natural pitting offer a raw appearance and will hide splashmarks well, but will be more difficult to keep clean.

74

paint it on

Ordinary latex/flat paint is not recommended for bathroom walls if there is a chance it will get splashed, as it will show stains and watermarks. Nor will it be resistant to steam and moist conditions, eventually peeling away and possibly succumbing to mildew. For this reason, if you are using paint in a bathroom, make sure it's a specialized paint suited for the purpose.

A better alternative is to choose a good-quality gloss or semigloss paint, which will be resistant to splashes and easy to wipe dry. However, such paints are not totally waterproof, so don't be tempted to use them as an alternative to tiles in wet areas. If your walls have imperfections, satin-finish paint is preferable to gloss, which highlights irregularities.

There is now a latex-based waterproofing paint that is easier to use than older versions; it comes only in white but can be colored with tinting colors. Paint with a mildew retardant is a good idea if your bathroom is very damp; however, the best way to deal with mildew is to prevent it by improving the ventilation.

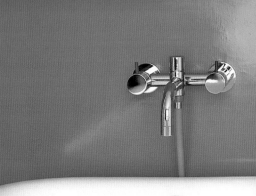

advantages

- Relatively inexpensive way of covering a large area
- Quick and easy to apply
- More durable than paint
- Easy to repaint if you want to change the color
- Light-reflecting finish expands the bathroom
- May inhibit mold or mildew

disadvantages

- Most kinds only water-resistant, not totally waterproof
- The sheen in the paint will highlight less-than-perfect walls
- Limited to a few specific ranges (therefore your color choice may be limited)
- Often more expensive than ordinary paints

75

polished plaster

Known also as stucco lustro, marmorino, or Venetian plaster, polished plaster is a centuries-old wall render that has traditionally adorned Italian palaces and churches. Its smooth, glossy look can be sumptuous and decorative; or with texture and pigmentation, it can appear rustic and weathered.

Polished plaster is particularly suited to bathrooms because it is hardwearing and waterproof. The base, made of lime, cement, and marble dust, is given added protection by layers of wax rubbed into the surface.

Application should be left to an expert, and you can specify different finishes. Polishing the surface brings the marble dust within the plaster to a smooth, high-gloss; but you can also ask for a pitted or dragged finish—for example, to add textural depth.

Historically, polished plaster took its hue from the natural, earthy colors of the Mediterranean region, but pigments can be added to tint the material to subtle or saturated colors. The colored finish is not uniform, but shows variations that add dimension to the room.

advantages

- Waterproof
- Durable
- Can be custom-colored
- Lots of different finishes

disadvantages

- Can be expensive
- Needs professional application

feet first

Flooring choices for bathrooms are wide ranging. You can opt for refined ceramic or earthy stone, traditional linoleum or high-tech vinyl, rustic cork or industrial rubber. Their looks and properties vary, but whatever material you choose, think about the practicalities as much as the aesthetics.

naked truth

Since you'll be walking on the bathroom floor with bare feet, how it feels to your skin is an important consideration—not only the texture, but the temperature, too. If you don't think you can cope with cold stone on a winter morning, perhaps underfloor heating is the answer.

slippery when wet

Take account of the fact that no matter how careful you are, some parts of your bathroom floor will get wet. Obviously, choose materials that are water-resistant, but make sure, too, that the surface is non-slip or incorporates a texture to give extra grip.

ups and downs

If the floor in your bathroom is a different material from that in the adjacent room, it may cause problems. For example, if you've laid underfloor heating and thick stone slabs, the bathroom floor might be several inches higher than the adjoining carpet. While a difference of a quarter-inch or so can be hidden with a standard threshold strip, unless you want to create a small step up into the bathroom (and risk stubbing your toe until you've learned the hard way), you'll need to smooth out any greater transitions. Ask your contractor (see 7) for solutions such as a sloped or custom-made threshold strip—or in extreme cases, you may need to raise the adjoining floor to minimize the difference. It's worth thinking about height differences when you're choosing your flooring.

keep it clean

The bathroom is where you go to get clean—not dirty. So you need a floor that is hygienic and easy to keep free of dirt and germs. For this reason, carpets are really not recommended for bathrooms. Yes, they feel nice underfoot, but they harbor bacteria, dead skin, and hair—and if they get wet too often, they will eventually get moldy and begin to smell.

what lies beneath

The success of your floor covering will depend on the preparation of the subfloor. If you're laying ceramic or stone, you must have a stable subfloor that will not flex or move (otherwise cracks will appear in your tiles on top), such as a concrete screed with a self-leveling compound. Vinyl and linoleum can be laid onto high-quality plywood, but it must be well fitted, smooth, and free of dirt, with no gaps between boards, or your flooring above will take on its defects. Your contractor or retailer should be able to advise on the most appropriate type of subflooring.

77 ceramic tiles

Although all ceramic tiles are extremely water-resistant, it is only when tiles are glazed that they become fully waterproof. Some types of floor tiles are unglazed and will have a degree of permeability.

Unglazed tiles include terracotta and other tiles made from a paste of natural clay, or shale, extruded into shape. Colors are limited to an earthy palette of red, brown, and gray. Terracotta has a rich burnt orange or red color, and the tiles are often hand-made, which gives them a raw and honest quality. Traditionally, terracotta tiles are waxed with beeswax to protect them, but there are modern sealants now available.

advantages of unglazed floor tiles

• Less slippery
• Extremely resistant to wear and abrasion
• The color is the same throughout (so chips won't show)

disadvantages of unglazed floor tiles

• Color and design options are limited
• Slightly porous unless sealed

The texture of your tiles, whether glazed or unglazed, is important. If the glaze is high gloss and the surface is smooth, the tile will be dangerously slippery when wet. An unglazed tile with a rough finish will have more traction.

five tile tips

1 • Ceramic tiles are hard and unforgiving underfoot. Anything you drop is likely to break, and may damage your tiles.
2 • Don't apply ceramic wall tiles to floors; they will be too thin to withstand people walking on them and will crack.
3 • If you're choosing a glazed ceramic tile, opt for a matte glaze and a slight texture to minimize risk of slipping.
4 • Mosaic tiles are good for floors, as the hundreds of grout lines give good traction underfoot.
5 • Grout on floors gets dirty. Consider using a waterproof epoxy grout rather than a more porous (though cheaper) cement-based grout.

stone

Whether your walls are surfaced with mini-mosaics or hefty slabs, the inherent solidity, longevity, and natural beauty of stone will be apparent.

granite

With its high quartz content, granite is the hardest stone cladding. This makes it a highly practical floor covering, though its density means it is extremely heavy.

marble

Marble's classical connotations are perfect for a traditional room. It is a soft and porous stone, which will stain and scratch unless properly cared for. It also tends to be slick when wet, so avoid highly polished slabs underfoot.

limestone

Limestone is a beautiful stone, with warm tones and uniform shading—but black-soled shoes, high heels, and water splashes will all take their toll. Most limestones are relatively soft and porous and will be unforgiving of daily abuse.

slate

Riven slate, which is cleaved rather than cut from the rock, has a wonderful irregular texture, which makes it extremely slip-resistant. In addition, slate has superb lateral strength, and a high degree of natural waterproofing.

other choices

Composites, which mix chips or granules of real stone with a bonding agent to produce a hard-wearing material, are easier to care for than natural stone. Terrazzo, for example, captures chips of granite or marble in polished mortar. You can even find realistic limestone look-alikes that compound limestone dust with resins.

four considerations

1 • The weight: The joists in your timber floor may need to be strengthened.

2 • The fragility: Make sure you prepare the subfloor correctly. Unless it's perfectly smooth and stable, you risk cracking the stones as you step on them.

3 • The temperature: Stone is affected by the temperature around it: If the subfloor is cold and damp, the stone will be cold and damp as well.

4 • The maintenance: For stone to keep its good looks, it needs to be cleaned regularly and resealed to maintain waterproofing.

vinyl and linoleum 79

Linoleum and vinyl, both manufactured waterproof floor coverings, are often mistaken for each other. They have many similarities in looks, applications, and inherent properties, but differ significantly in construction.

Vinyl truly is a synthetic material. Made from PVC (with some filler compounds in cheaper brands), vinyl is resilient, waterproof, hard-wearing, hygienic, and easy to clean: all properties that make it an excellent covering for bathroom floors.

You can choose between sheet or tile vinyl. The sheet form is unwieldy and best fitted by an expert, but has the advantage of being seam-free. Tiles are more manageable and can even be fitted by a proficient amateur. However, care must be taken to make sure the tiles butt tightly up against each other and that adhesive seals the gaps. As water can seep between the tiles if they are not fitted correctly, some manufacturers will guarantee the product only if installed by an approved fitter, which can add to the expense. You can get self-adhesive vinyl tiles, which are cheaper, but these are more likely to move and are less waterproof.

Both cushioned and uncushioned vinyl are available. The latter is softer underfoot, but will show any marks and dents from high heels or furniture legs, or if anything sharp is dropped on it.

While linoleum is also man-made, the substances used are natural, not synthetic. The material takes its name from linseed oil, one of its prime ingredients, with others being cork, wood flour, resins, chalk, limestone, and natural pigments. Sheet linoleum is on pliable jute backing, and the tile variety is on rigid polyester.

Linoleum shares vinyl's easy-clean properties, and is also hardwearing. In fact, over time, exposure to air hardens it and increases its durability, though it remains relatively quiet underfoot. But unlike vinyl, linoleum is environmentally friendly, being made of recyclable and sustainable raw materials.

And its linseed oil content has an additional benefit: The continuous oxidization of the oil produces a bactericidal effect, which makes it extremely hygienic in the bathroom. What's more, linoleum is anti-static, repelling dust and so being easier to clean.

ten reasons to buy vinyl or linoleum

1 • Waterproof
2 • Durable
3 • Easy-clean smooth surface
4 • Quiet and warm underfoot
5 • Can be laid in seam-free sheets
6 • Hygienic
7 • Vast variety of colors and designs (including authentic imitations of stone)
8 • Anti-static (linoleum only)
9 • Antibacterial (linoleum only)
10 • Eco-friendly (linoleum only)

but be careful with

• Cushioned materials (will show dents)
• Cheaper materials (will show wear/be less waterproof)
• Tiles (will allow water to seep between if not fitted properly)
• Sheet (needs expert fitting, and there may be more wastage—plus, if you have a large bath, you might need a join)

copycat

With vinyl and linoleum you have the possibility of replica ceramic tiles, wood, stone, or even metal flooring that offers the aesthetic benefits of those materials without the issues of maintenance or waterproofing. Modern technology makes these imitations extremely realistic. Or, you can take advantage of other technological advances and choose a digital design with holographic qualities, highly saturated colors, or subtle textures.

wood—and grass! 80

Bathrooms often have a cold, clinical appearance, which can be tempered by the introduction of warm and organic materials, such as wood. The look can be as rustic or as refined as you wish, from wide-board oak to open-grained tropical woods, or narrow planks of elegant maple or beech.

• Solid hardwood: Planks or strips of real wood. It's expensive, but beautiful; may warp in humidity, but can be protected with coats of lacquer; will mark over time, but can be sanded and re-lacquered
• Engineered flooring: A veneer of real wood bonded to layers of chipboard. It's reasonably priced and looks good; more stable than solid wood, especially if lacquered, but may still warp in moist conditions; will mark, but can be sanded and re-lacquered only a limited number of times
• Laminate flooring: A photographic reproduction of wood bonded to layers of chipboard or high-density fiberboard and covered with a clear protective layer. It's the most affordable option; certain brands are suited to bathrooms and even come with a guarantee; less susceptible to marking or denting than real wood

house of bamboo

Often mistaken for a wood, though in fact it's a grass, bamboo has become big news for bathrooms. Layers of bamboo strips are laminated under high pressure to produce a flooring material that looks like wood but has properties that make it much more suitable for bathrooms. It is much more stable than wood flooring, and won't shrink or swell noticeably in a moist atmosphere.

With its distinctive linear markings, bamboo is unusual and attractive. Its typical color is honey blond, but it can be pressure steamed for a darker shade. Being plentiful it is also a very environmentally friendly product.

cork

81

Cork flooring is undergoing something of a design revival, perhaps due to its good-value price and its eco-friendliness. Its new look combines warm charm with contemporary aesthetics.

Consisting of about 50% air, cork offers excellent shock absorbency and soundproofing, but is permeable to water unless sealed. Some companies supply cork tiles with a coating of durable, waterproof (though not eco-friendly) plastic. Otherwise, your floor will require four or five layers of sealant. Once sealed, cork is easy to clean, needing only a quick sweep and a damp mop.

You can find pigmented cork that takes the color palette beyond the neutral browns, or even cork-backed tiles finished with patterned or photographic digital images protected by a plastic coating.

rubber

82

Hard-wearing and waterproof, industrial-style rubber flooring has now moved into bathrooms. You can find synthetic, natural, and recycled rubber flooring, all with similar properties: warmth, softness, and hygiene. Tiles are easier to lay than rubber on a roll, but will have more joins where water could penetrate. An alternative is a poured rubber floor, but this will need professional installation.

Because rubber becomes slick if wet, look for a textured anti-skid surface, such as a pattern of studs, dimples, or tread plate effect. You'll have a huge color choice, from industrial gray to marbled mixes of bright hues.

Keep your rubber flooring shining with applications of specialized polish, clean it with a damp mop, and buff it dry afterward.

let there be light

A successful lighting plan should harmonize so well with the way you use the room that you scarcely notice how effective it is. You're more likely to comment on poor illumination than good.

laying down the ground rules

Before you can begin to plan your lighting, you must finalize your bathroom design (see 11). After all, it's no good installing mirror lighting and then realizing that you want the mirror on the opposite wall. The position of the bathtub, sink, and shower will guide your plans, as will any special features, such as recesses or alcoves.

variations on a theme

A single pendant light in the center of the ceiling provides the most basic illumination. It might even seem sufficient for a small bathroom. But how much more visually exciting—and how much more useful—to have a variety of lighting, such as uplights, downlights, and wall washers. Layers of lighting, some diffused and some directed, make every area of the bathroom accessible.

feeling flexible

Having decided you'll have more than one light source in the bathroom, make the decision to have separate controls for different lighting. That way, you can decide to switch off the bright halogen downlights if you want to lie back in the tub and relax—no getting dazzled when you look at the ceiling. Instead, turn on some mood-enhancing uplights or an accent light.

If you have a dimmer switch installed, you'll be able to control the ambiance even more. And a dimmer will be especially useful when you're entering the bathroom from a dark bedroom in the middle of the night or early in the morning, allowing your eyes to adjust slowly.

sources of light

• Natural light is the best source of illumination, though in bathrooms it will often be diffused by a window treatment or blocked altogether, which means you'll have to resort to artificial illumination even during the daytime.

• Incandescent bulbs are the most common form of domestic lighting. The bulb contains a filament, usually made of tungsten; when electricity passes through this filament, the filament glows, producing a warm-toned light. For a soft effect, choose a pearl incandescent bulb.

• Halogen light also uses a tungsten filament, but in this type of lamp, halogen gas is trapped within the bulb, and reacts with the heated filament to produce a much whiter and brighter light.

• Fluorescent light has a bad reputation in bathrooms. It's generally unflattering and flickering—not what you want as you peer in the mirror. However, a new generation of compact fluorescents are flicker-free, and some even mimic natural daylight.

safe and sound

It's obvious, but it bears repeating that water and electricity are a dangerous mix. For this reason, building codes (which differ from one locality to another) are in place to protect you. Involve a qualified electrician in your lighting design, and he or she will be able to advise you on your plans and even carry out the installation (see 10). A few general points to bear in mind are

• Water-resistant lights: Any fixture that might get wet will need to be sealed. You can get fully waterproof lights for shower areas, for example, and water-resistant lights for other areas of the bathroom. If you choose a pendant light, you might not think it needs to be water-resistant. However, even one splash of cold water can cause a hot bulb to shatter, so it's worth protecting the bulb.

• Switches: In some countries you can't have switches in the bathroom (only pull-cords). Check your local building codes about different types of switches and where you're allowed to position them (see 10).

84 ambient lighting

Obviously, the primary function of lighting in the bathroom is to allow us to see; but that basic fact aside, illumination can also be used to set a mood and even as a decorative effect. Light can create shadows, highlight textures, cast patterns, and add a new dimension to a surface. So take both practical and aesthetic functions into account when you plan your lighting.

three questions to ask yourself

1 • How much natural light enters the bathroom? Is it via a window or a skylight? Does it enter the whole year? Do you currently block it with a window treatment?

2 • Do you use the bathroom in the dark hours of the morning? During the day? Late at night?

3 • Do you want your bathroom to wake you up and refresh you? Do you like to relax and unwind in the bathroom? Does your mood vary?

Obviously, if the bathroom has no window at all or if you have to totally block it to stop neighbors from seeing in, you'll need to create some "daylight" by artificial means. A skylight is perhaps the best means of letting natural light into the room, but at night, you'll still need to switch on a light.

Most people will use the bathroom at different times of day; early morning before they leave for work, late at night before going to bed. In the morning, you usually want to be refreshed—but not blinded—by light. In the evening, you want to be able to soak in a tub with atmospheric lighting to soothe you.

There's no hard and fast rule about how many lights you need for a particular size of bathroom, nor how bright or how dim they need to be. But in general, err on the generous side, and build in flexibility so that you can alter the level of illumination—and the areas that are illuminated—according to your need.

Uplights are an excellent means of creating a sense of space. Reflected off a white-painted ceiling, they seem to heighten the bathroom. They can be wall-mounted or set into a surface such as a shelf or even the floor. On the floor, they'll need to be in fully sealed casings in case of water spillages. Also, choose a low-voltage light, which won't get too hot, as you'll probably walk over it with bare feet. And finally, make sure the light is positioned so it doesn't shine directly into your eyes (for example, as you bend over the sink).

Balance uplights with downlights, such as pendant spotlights and recessed halogen spots. Position one over the bathtub or sink for the effect of light on rippling water. A series of recessed ceiling lights close to the edge of the ceiling act as wall-washers, creating a scalloped pattern of light arches on the wall.

task lighting

Task lighting is the most useful type of illumination, and in bathrooms it usually centers on the mirror to help with general grooming, as well as more specific activities such as shaving, applying makeup, and putting in contact lenses.

mirror lighting

You want to be able to peer closely at your reflection without your face being shadowed. Light from a single direction, such as a downlight over the basin, will cast shadows in your eye sockets and below your nose.

If a downlight is all you have, at least angle it toward the mirror. Light will be reflected back on your face and will minimize shadows. A better solution is to provide even, diffused light from either side, such as two halogen strip lights (or incandescent for a warmer glow). These can also be balanced by a downlight above.

Look for mirrors with integrated lighting—some even have a full perimeter of recessed light, which makes sure that the face is illuminated from every angle.

three other places for task lighting

1 • The bathtub: if you like to lie in the tub and read, you'll need a good source of light above your head.
2 • The shower: recessed shower enclosures can be terribly dark and dreary. A fully sealed overhead light is essential.
3 • Storage units: make sure light is directed inside hard-to-see places, so you can reach into drawers and cabinets and easily find what you're looking for.

86 feature lighting

As its name suggests, feature lighting in the bathroom is intended to illuminate specific aspects of the design. You might want strategically placed lights to draw attention to special features, from a monolithic bathtub in the center of the room to a small ornament on a display shelf.

the bathtub

Consider paneling the bathtub with translucent acrylic and backlighting this with fully protected strip lighting. The effect can be particularly striking if colored acrylic is used. Another option is a perimeter of light at the base of a freestanding bathtub, created using recessed strips or even a ropelight. This will give the visual illusion of the bathtub floating in space.

the sink

Light directed at, and bouncing off, a high-gloss white ceramic sink is not as effective as light actually directed through a sink. With a glass bowl (or even just a glass surround), use recessed and waterproofed under-lighting to create a wonderful ethereal glow around the glass.

glass screens

As with sinks, glass screens, or panels, are ideal candidates for feature lighting. A wall of glass blocks or a shower screen of green-tinged frosted glass can be up-lit or down-lit. The light streams along and through the glass and hangs tantalizingly on the edges.

display shelves and alcoves

Passing light, from either above or below, through a series of glass shelves brings a stunning luminance to the display area. You might also want to highlight any alcoves or recesses in the bathroom wall.

87 the heat is on

As you step out of a hot bath or steamy shower, you want the air around you to be comfortably warm. Your existing heating system may be doing this job perfectly well, but if you're thinking of installing a new system, you might consider installing a radiant heating system. Also called underfloor, or infloor heating, this type of heating has long been popular in Europe and is beginning to catch on in the United States, too.

5 ideas

now you see it . . .

Heating appliances can be discreet—like baseboard heaters and forced-air grates—or "in your face"—like the old steam radiator, which has recently become a design statement. Underfloor heating, on the other hand, is hidden beneath your floor finish, and you can't tell it's there until you walk barefoot over it.

saving space?

If you live in an old house or apartment and are stuck with a bulky radiator, put a shelf over it and use this for bathroom accessories. Some clean, neatly folded hand towels and washcloths could make an attractive display and free up some cabinet space.

economic situation

Underfloor heating gives out radiant heat, transmitting heat directly to cooler surfaces, such as your body. Most other systems heat by convection: warm air rises, becomes cold and falls, creating air currents and hot and cold patches. Because radiant heat is more effective, it can be used at lower temperatures and can be cheaper to run than other systems.

fresh air

Underfloor heating doesn't create air movement, so it's a healthier option than other types of heating for asthmatics or anyone who is susceptible to allergies. This is because there's no continuous circulation of dust in the air.

maintenance

Other heating appliances are easier to access than underfloor heating. However, with electric underfloor heating most manufacturers offer a guarantee and can pinpoint faults, so only a few tiles need to be lifted. A leak in a water-based system is much more of a problem.

underfloor heating

There are two main types of underfloor heating: hydronic and electric.

hydronic

A hydronic system consists of a network of hot water pipes laid in a concrete screed floor. If you're simply redecorating a bathroom, a hydronic system probably isn't suitable for the following reasons:
- it would elevate the floor by about 6 inches (creating a big step at the threshold);
- the concrete would be too heavy for your joists;
- it's very expensive to install.

However, if you're building a new house and want underfloor heating throughout, a hot-water system is the best solution (it's cheap to run in the long term).

electric

Electrical underfloor heating comes in three main forms:
- Foil mats: Panels of extremely thin, tightly woven carbon or metal mesh.
- Cable mats: Electrical cables are set at regular intervals within a fiberglass mesh. They require a regular-shaped room, as the cabling can't be cut.
- Cabling: Electrical cabling gives more flexibility and so can reach areas that the cable mats can't.

Foil mats are low voltage and have low heat output, which means they can be used with wood, laminate, and vinyl floors, as well as stone and ceramic. They don't produce enough heat to be the sole source in the room, whereas cable mats and cabling can be either the primary or secondary heat source in the room, depending on the heat output. The higher outputs are best suited to stone and ceramic flooring.

Electrical systems are just a fraction of an inch thick and can be taped onto the subfloor and then covered with the floor adhesive, before the tiles are laid. The systems are insulated and waterproofed for safety.

radiators

If your house is old, the bathroom may contain an old-fashioned bulky radiator that takes up a lot of space. One option is to replace it with a panel radiator. These slim-line fixtures, long used in Britain, are relatively unobtrusive. But there are more interesting options.

modern

Contemporary designs include ladder rails and loops, curves, and squares. Many styles double up as towel warmers, although their primary function is to heat the room. The latest trends are
• Metallic finishes such as matte or polished chrome to coordinate with faucets and other accessories
• Tall, thin, vertical designs—wall mounted to make floors easier to clean and free up space for the bathtub and other fixtures
• Integrated accessories such as mirrors, bathrobe hooks, and even shelving

traditional

If you're going for a traditional look, you might hold on to that bulky radiator—they're now back in fashion! An alternative style is the ball-jointed ladder in brass, nickel, or combined finishes (see 55), with cross handles or ceramic valves to add an authentic look. Like its contemporary cousins, it can be wall mounted and is more space saving than a column style of radiator.

hot enough?

Estimating the optimum radiator size and heat output needed for a room is a job best left to a professional. Precise calculations can take into account not only the room size but also the size of windows and the number and area of outside walls.

fuel for thought

Most radiators can be plumbed into your heating system, but some are electric only, and others offer the flexibility of dual-fuel.

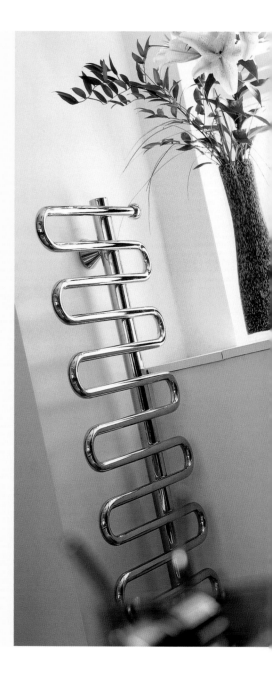

towel warmers

90

In Europe, where central heating has been widely adopted only in recent years, the towel-warming rail has long provided a solution to the problem of cold, damp bath towels. In fact, these appliances make towels so deliciously warm that they are often installed in centrally heated homes, including, these days, some of those in the United States.

Some towel warmers are connected to a hydronic heating system, so may substitute for a radiator; others are operated electrically. The latter option is especially practical if you have a forced-air heating and air-conditioned system. You can enjoy a cool bathroom in summer along with a warm towel when you step out of the tub or shower.

doubling up

towel warmers and radiators

If your bathroom is already well heated, a towel warmer might seem superfluous; towels will get dry in fairly short order if placed over an ordinary rod. But if you like the idea of warm towels, you could install a warmer and then reduce the heat output of the existing radiator or vent. Some manufacturers (check the Internet) make combined panel radiator-towel warmers. If the bathroom is small and not drafty, you might even find that a good-sized towel warmer would provide enough heat all by itself to keep the bathroom comfortably warm.

towel warmers and underfloor heating

If you have radiant underfloor, or infloor, heating, a small, electrically-run towel warmer will provide just enough heat to warm towels without overheating the bathroom. And you can pamper your bare feet and the rest of your body at the same time.

size matters

When choosing a towel warmer, take into account the size of your towels. If you have large bath sheets, choose a wider model, so the towels won't have to be folded up too much to fit on it.

finishing touches

01

The smallest details really do make a difference. If you've spent time, energy, and money creating your perfect bathroom, it's a shame if the design falls at the last hurdle. So when you're redecorating your bathroom, remember the small, but practical, accessories that will make life easier—and your bathroom truly perfect.

toothbrush holder

A rack or cup, either wall-mounted or freestanding, offers room to store several toothbrushes—and the toothpaste too. But be sure to check whether the holes will take your usual brand of toothbrush: sometimes, chunky handles don't fit through.

toilet brush

An essential item, the toilet brush, comes in all styles, from sleek polished chrome to funky colorful plastic. Look for models that hide the brush itself from sight and have an easy-to-clean interior and exterior.

5
details

soap dish or dispenser

If you use a bar of soap, keep it on hand in a rack-style or ridged dish that will allow the underside of the soap to dry. For liquid soap, consider a wall-mounted pump dispenser, which clears the counter of yet another bottle.

bathrobe hooks

Your dressing gown needs a home, and a robe hook on the back of the bathroom door is the perfect place.

towel hoops or rails

If your sink doesn't offer an integrated rack, make sure you provide a convenient hoop or rail to hold the hand towel. Of course, you'll also need plenty of rails to hold bath towels and washcloths. For a bit of luxury, install a towel warmer.

92 mirrors

In a bathroom, mirrors perform several functions. One is, obviously, as a looking glass. But as well as this, a mirror is a useful means of enhancing light in a dark bathroom, and it also serves to visually increase the dimensions of a small space.

up close and personal

Fixed flush to the wall or on the front of a cabinet, your mirror needs to offer good balanced lighting so your face isn't in shadow, which means you'll need light at least from either side, if not all directions.

For "close-up work," such as putting on eye makeup, plucking hairs, or putting in contact lenses, a supplementary magnifying mirror with integrated illumination is an extremely useful addition. Fitted to a flexible stem, it can be angled to best advantage.

optical illusions

An expanse of mirror can be positioned to reflect natural light, or even artificial light sources, into dark corners. Not only will a wall-to-wall mirror above the bathtub achieve this, but it will also seem to double the size of your room. Be sure, though, that you'll feel comfortable with a large mirror in the bathroom; not everyone likes to see themselves so exposed.

steamy mirrors

One problem with mirrors in a bathroom is that they tend to become fogged up when you have a steamy shower, or even a hot bath. An anti-condensation coating helps reduce the problem, but the best solution is to raise the temperature of the mirrored surface so steam can't condense there. Some mirrors come with an integrated heating element, and you can also buy thin heating pads to fix behind wall mirrors, which take the chill off the surface.

index

acknowledgments

Author's acknowledgements

My thanks go to Jane O'Shea, Hilary Mandleberg, Helen Lewis, Paul Welti and Samantha Rolfe at Quadrille for all their help and hard work in seeing this book come to completion. And, of course, to my husband, Michael, for his support in my freelance career.

Picture credits

1 Ray Main/Mainstream; 7 Ray Main/Mainstream/Arch Julie Richards@msn.com; 8-9 Ray Main/Mainstream; 10-11 Ray Main/Mainstream/ Dev Martin Lee Associates; 12-13 Ray Main/Mainstream/Hemming-way designs; 14-15 Ray Main/ Mainstream/Arch Julie Richards@msn.com; 16 Ray Main/Mainstream; 18-19 Ray Main/Mainstream/Developer Leeds Loft Co.; 20 Main/ Mainstream/Guinevere; 21 Ray Main/Mainstream/MMR Architects; 22 Ray Main/ Mainstream/Architect Spencer Fung; 23 Ray Main/ Mainstream; 24 Ray Main/ Mainstream; 24-25 Ray Main/ Mainstream; 26 Ray Main/ Mainstream; 27 Ray Main/ Mainstream; 29 Ray Main/ Mainstream/Designer Roger Oates; 30-31 Ray Main/ Mainstream; 31 Ray Main/ Mainstream/Hazlitts; 32-33 Ray Main/Mainstream; 35 Ray Main/Mainstream; 26-37 Ray Main/Mainstream/C2 Architects; 37 Ray Main/ Mainstream; 38 above Ray Main/Mainstream; 38 below Ray Main/Mainstream/ Developers Candy&Candy; 40 Ray Main/Mainstream/ Architects Gregory Phillips; 41 Ideal-Standard Idealcast roll top bath www.ideal-standard. co.uk; 42 Ray Main/ Mainstream; 42-43 inset Ray Main/Mainstream/Patel Taylor Architects; 43 Ray Main/ Mainstream/Developer Candy&Candy; 44-45 Ray Main/Mainstream/Architect Neil Fletchers; 46-47 Ray Main/Mainstream; 48 Alchemy showerhead by Sottini (an Ideal-Standard company) www.sottini.co.uk; 49 Darren Chung/Mainstream; 50 Ray Main/Mainstream; 51 Ray Main/Mainstream/ Developer Candy&Candy; 52 below Darren Chung/ Mainstream; 52-3 above Ray Main/ Mainstream/Architect Simon Conder; 53 below Ray Main/ Mainstream/John Minshaw Designs; 54-55 Ray Main/ Mainstream; 56 below Ray Main/Mainstream/ Designer Andrew Martin; 56 above Ray Main/Mainstream; 57 centre Ray Main/ Mainstream/ Candy&Candy; 57 right Ray Main/ Mainstream; 57 left Darren Chung/Mainstream/C2 Design; 59 Ray Main/ Mainstream/John Minshaw Designs; 60-61 Ray Main/ Mainstream/London & Country Homes; 62 top Ray Main/ Mainstream/Designer Paul Daly; 62 below Ray Main/ Mainstream; 63 above Ray Main/Mainstream; 63 below Ray Main/Mainstream/ The Rookery; 64 Ray Main/ Mainstream/Developers Candy&Candy; 65 Dreamworks three-hole basin mixer by Michael Graves for Dornbracht www.dornbracht.com; 66 Ray Main/Mainstream; 67 Sottini Cresta suite www.sottini.co.uk; 68-69 Ray Main/Mainstream/ Mary Thum Architects; 68-69 inset Ray Main/Mainstream/ Arch Wells Mackereth; 70-71 Ray Main/Mainstream; 72 Ray Main/Mainstream; 73 Ray Main/Mainstream/Architect Sabrina Foster; 74 Ray Main/ Mainstream; 75 Ray Main/ Mainstream; 76-7 main & inset Ray Main/Mainstream/ Abraham & Thakore; 78-79 Ray Main/Mainstream; 79 Ray Main/Mainstream; 80 Ray Main/Mainstream/Architect Charles Rutherford; 80-81 Ray Main/Mainstream; 81 Ray Main/Mainstream; 82-83 main Ray Main/Mainstream; 82-3 inset Ray Main/Mainstream; 84-85 Ray Main/Mainstream; 87 Darren Chung/Mainstream/ Bathaus; 88-89 Ray Main/ Mainstream; 89 Ray Main/ Mainstream; 90-91 Ray Main/ Mainstream/John Minshaw Designs; 91 Ray Main/ Mainstream/Designer Gianni Cinnali; 92 Darren Chung/ Mainstream/Bathaus; 93 Ray Main/Mainstream; 94-95 Ray Main/Mainstream; 96-97 Ray Main/Mainstream; 98 Ray Main/Mainstream; 99 Ray Main/Mainstream/Designer Nick Allen; 100-101 Ray Main/ Mainstream; 102-103 Darren Chung/Mainstream; 103 Ray Main/Mainstream; 104 Ray Main/Mainstream; 105 Ray Main/Mainstream; 106 Ray Main/Mainstream; 107 Ray Main/Mainstream/Designer Catherine Memmi; 108 Ray Main/Mainstream/MMR Architects; 109 Ray Main/ Mainstream; 111 Ray Main/ Mainstream; 112-113 Ray Main/Mainstream/Gregory Phillips; 114-115 Darren Chung/Mainstream/C2 Design; 116 Ray Main/ Mainstream; 117 Ray Main/ Mainstream